JOHNNY CASH
AT FOLSOM PRISON

ALSO BY MICHAEL STREISSGUTH

Ring of Fire: The Johnny Cash Reader (editor)
Eddy Arnold: Pioneer of the Nashville Sound
Like a Moth to a Flame: The Jim Reeves Story
Voices of the Country: Interview with Classic Country Performers

JOHNNY CASH
AT FOLSOM PRISON
THE MAKING OF A MASTERPIECE

MICHAEL STREISSGUTH

DA CAPO PRESS | A MEMBER OF THE PERSEUS BOOKS GROUP

Lyrics from "Folsom Prison Blues" by John R. Cash, copyright © 1956 (renewed 1984) by House of Cash Inc. All rights resereved. Reprinted by permission of the estate of Johnny Cash.

Cataloging-in-Publication data for this book is available from the Library of Congress

First Da Capo Press edition 2004
ISBN 0-306-81338-6
Published by Da Capo Press
A Member of the Perseus Books Group
www.dacapopress.com

Da Capo Press books are available at special discounts for bulk purchases in the U.S. by corporations, institutions, and other organizations. For more information, please contact the Special Markets Department at the Perseus Books Group, 11 Cambridge Center, Cambridge, MA 02142, or call (800) 255-1514 or (617) 252-5298, or e-mail *special.markets@perseusbooks.com*.

Design by Cooley Design Lab

1 2 3 4 5 6 7 8 9 — 07 06 05 04

For Mom and Dad

(Photo by Jim Marshall)

CONTENTS

ACKNOWLEDGMENTS

Four major regions of the United States helped one Syracusan write a book about a Johnny Cash album: East Coast, West Coast, South, and Midwest. Although personal animosity may linger, sectionalism is dead.

On the East Coast: Leslie Bailey Streissguth, my wife and first editor; Karl Streissguth, my father, who found the *Johnny Cash At Folsom Prison* LP on one of his regular digs through used vinyl; Dan McIntyre, the neighborhood Dylanologist; Wayne Stevens, Tarzan Brothers drummer and Le Moyne College interlibrary loan commander; Ben Schafer, my editor at Da Capo and a great guy; Jim Fitzgerald, my agent; Michael Poulin and Gretchen Pearson, both of whom searched for the *Los Angeles Times;* Steve Andreassi of the IUP Lodge and Convocation Center in Hoboken; Steve Berkowitz, Joe Lizzi, Don Devito, John Jackson, Nick Shaffran, Denise Cabrera, all of Sony Music; Jim Irwin of Sundazed Records; Charles Cronin of the Arthur W. Diamond Law Library at Columbia University; Suzanne Eggleston Lovejoy of the Yale Music Library; Ed Brown, Sheila Chlanda; Denise Gasiorowski; Steve Govoni; Robert Osterberg, Hopeton Smalling; Stephanie Venagas; David Streissguth; Monica Sondej.

On the West Coast: Jim Marshall, who photographed rock and roll history; Lt. Tom Ayers, who toured me around Folsom Prison; Jim Brown, John Fratis, John Moore, all retired Folsom corrections officers; Terry Thornton of the California Department of Corrections; Jeff Crawford of the California State Archives in Sacramento; Julie Bowen and Karen Mehring of the Folsom Historical Society; Lou Robin who managed Johnny Cash for more than 30 years; George Horn of Fantasy Records; Sioban Spain of the *Los Angeles Times*; Millard Dedmon; Marshall Diemert; Wornall Farr; Gordon Henry; Bruce Jenkins; Gordon Jenkins, Jr.; Lloyd "Coach" Kelley; Tom Noonan; Cy Mitchell; Clarence Obitz; Noel and Roger Wise.

In the South: Dr. William Thomas of Harrisonburg, Virginia; Marty Stuart, who's been set ablaze by Johnny Cash; Dawn Oberg of the Country Music Foundation Library and Archives in Nashville; Kelly Hancock at House of Cash; Alanna Nash who always has an ear for the listening; Joe Casey; Marshall Grant; Earl Green; Bob Johnston; Frank Jones; Don Reid; Harold Reid; Patricia Sanders; Rusty Courtney; Keith Sherley; Bob Sullivan; Ruth White.

In the Midwest: Peter C. Cavanagh; Gene Dennonovich; Mervin Forbes.

Finally, I can't forget Stephen Miller, author of *Johnny Cash: The Life of an American Icon,* who helped me confirm details regarding Cash's 1966 show at Folsom Prison.

INTRODUCTION

Lately I've been dreaming about Cash.

A few midnights ago in the ethereal, I chided him about "Hey Porter," side B of his first Sun Records release. *How much longer will it be/'Til we cross that Mason Dixon line?* "Hey Cash, where was that Southbound guy coming from? Was he on holiday break from Yale?" Cash sneered at me. "Be careful," he warned in a voice that came from some ancient hollow. "Or I'll sic David Allan Coe on you."

Our next visit rambled through the night, one of those dreams that persists even after you've wakened a time or two to comfort your child or gather up your blanket. We were making our way around a sprawling lake or harbor in the shadow of a sky-scrapered city. Seattle? Chicago? Salt Lake City? We came to a channel that broke the shore. I moved to cross, over a bridge or by ferry. But he raised his hand as if to say he could go no farther.

Last night, he appeared in the distance, perhaps in television's grayish haze. Dressed in a white shirt and blue jeans, or maybe it was a white suit like Bob Dylan wore at the Isle of Wight festival in 1969, he was visiting scenes from his life. I struggled through the fog, to a place where he greeted me. He knew I wanted to talk about stops on his way, to see, to learn. We time traveled, hovering about scenes from his life that seemed ripped from a dog-eared history book. We paused at his childhood home in Dyess, Arkansas, where Mississippi River floods tested his family's resilience—and where he agonized over his older brother Jack's violent death after a sawmill accident. Was his cracker box house freshly painted or splintered with age? I cannot remember. But we vanished from Arkansas as quickly as we had arrived, landing somewhere in the country where we ambled up a dirt road like two ol' boys with fishing poles. It was Poor Valley in southwestern

Virginia, home of the Carters, country music's seminal family. We climbed up from our dusty path to meet June Carter Cash, all in flowers, who left a simmering pot in the kitchen to welcome us at her door; she spoke about her glorious Elysium.

Later in the night, I stood with my somber guide at the edge of a field sizing up a rusted lump of Plymouth sedan, which carried the barnstorming singer and his Tennessee Two during the 1950s. Among golden alfalfa grass that rustled in the wind and a few leafy hickory trees, Cash uncorked his memories. But the rest of the dream eludes me. Did we visit Sun Records? The Ryman Auditorium? The Newport Folk Festival?

Perhaps tomorrow night we will go to Folsom Prison.

I visited Folsom alone in June of 2003, three months before Cash died and 35 years after he marched somberly through the gates of the loathsome Gothic compound to record an album for Columbia Records. As the guards patted me down and examined my shoes, belt, and wallet, I wondered if I'd see glimmers of that long ago day in 1968, or of Cash himself. He'd visited on at least two other occasions—in 1966 and 1977—but as I was ushered through the labyrinth of corridors I discerned no trace of Cash or his communion with the prisoners. The inmates whom I saw huddled at the foot of towering white cellblocks were not of Cash's generation; they were the characters of Tupac Shakur's and Snoop Dogg's ghetto verse. And in the cavernous dining hall where he and his band thundered in 1968 there were no plaques, no markers, no echoes.

It was only when I passed back through the prison's high gates that Cash appeared. A few retired corrections officers who run a small Folsom museum immediately outside the prison walls keep the flame of Johnny Cash. They had hung on the wall poster-sized photos of Cash's 1968 concert, and like old schoolmasters, reminded me that Cash had never served time in Folsom. "He played here with the Perkins brothers, you know," they added in earnest, unaware that guitarists Luther and Carl, who backed Cash

that day, merely shared a surname, not parentage. "The concert was in dining room #1 ... or was it dining room #2?" It was in dining room #2. While
we talked, visitors to the museum glanced at the encased shanks and other
relics of a hard place, but they lingered in front of the images of Cash.
Synonymous with Folsom, the fabled troubadour was their strongest association with the reformatory.

An infamous prison since the first convict was admitted in the 1880s,
Cash's hit single "Folsom Prison Blues" (of 1955 and 1968) and his recorded
concert there had bought it international notoriety. And Folsom had
responded in kind. When Cash showed up at the prison in 1968 with crates
of recording equipment and the hard hunger of a struggling salesman, he
was coming off a five-year commercial lull during which drugs ravaged him
even as he matured artistically. But Cash lurched awake when the album he
recorded there, *Johnny Cash At Folsom Prison,* hit the record bins and began
moving like the 20TH Century Limited. What the NBC-TV stage in
Burbank would be for Elvis Presley in December of 1968, Folsom Prison
was for Johnny Cash in January of 1968.

The album signaled a resurgence that redefined his place in music history. Henceforth, in the eyes of everybody, he would once and for all be the
poet for the little man (which he'd always been, anyway) and all would
regard him a leviathan figure in popular music. The album opened vast commercial fields to Cash and escorted country music—his home base—to new
heights.

Among everything else and perhaps above everything else, *Folsom* was
also a social statement on behalf of disenfranchised peoples, as potent as
any such statement in the roiling 1960s, for by appearing in front of
America's modern-day lepers and recording and releasing what came of it,
he unapologetically told his listeners that these locked-away men deserved
the compassion, if not the liberation, that the 1960s offered. He used his art
as a battering ram to smash through conventional notions of prisoners and
prisons. None of Cash's peers in popular music ever dared to so brazenly
wield their music, not Dylan, not Zappa, not the Beatles, not Country Joe
McDonald, not Crosby, Stills, Nash and (or) Young, not any big-selling artist

who composed and performed so-called protest music in the 1960s. Transcending the decade of its birth, the album still resonates in the early 21ST century, when criminal justice remains anything but rational and man has never appeared more insensitive to his fellow man. *Johnny Cash At Folsom Prison*'s unique and powerful compassion for humanity, coupled with its pivotal role in the career of Cash and country music, grant it a place among the most significant albums of the 1960s, if not of the past 50 years—although it's rarely recognized as such, stacked as it is under at least two dozen more fêted albums primarily from the psychedelic age.

The story of this oft-underrated record begins on the doorstep of the rock era, many years before its 1968 recording, in blood-sodden postwar Germany, where hard currency for a defeated Nazi soldier or a restless American serviceman was his uncertain dream.

To the impassioned will all things be possible—Thornton Wilder.

0001

Landsberg, Germany must have seemed a far-off outpost to an 18-year-old from a patch of cotton in Dyess, Arkansas. Sunk deep in Bavaria near the Austrian border, Adolf Hitler had plotted his thousand-year Reich from a cell in the city's prison, but when young J. R. Cash landed there in 1951 the dictator's grand design was rubble. Six years earlier, the U.S. Army's 12TH Armored Division had rolled into Landsberg to find clustered around the city 11 concentration camps where thousands had died. The victims lay scattered on the ground like the charred beams and rafters of a burnt-down home. The survivors—bruised, starved, and clad in dirty striped uniforms— told of a final slaughter that occurred hours before the Americans arrived. Determined to impress on Landsbergers the shame of their Nazi complicity, the Army rounded them up and forced them to bury the human carnage that had piled up in their midst.

In 1951, still burdened by the sins of Hitler's barbarism, Landsberg was a gloomy, leaden place, especially to a saucer-eyed boy from the lap of post-war America. Cash could only have marveled as he surveyed the empty camps and heard the strident and strange German language, which until then had only been staccato enemy gibberish in American newsreels.

This guarded though innocent face with its droopy nose peered warily at his new home: Landsberg's snow and cold, far from the rime of Southern winters, subdued him, and his fellow servicemen's drinking offended his Baptist sensibilities. He chafed also at the tedium of his job deciphering Soviet code, which later drove him to toss a typewriter out the window. (An understanding supervisor granted Cash a few days' leave, sending him off with a bottle of pills to soothe the nervous strain.)

His mind raced and often turned toward home, although he hardly missed the family farm of his childhood—he'd been trying to flee from there since high school graduation, first to the manufacturing jungle of Pontiac, Michigan, and then to the air force. Instead, his mind turned to Vivian Liberto, a slender young woman with a magnetic smile from San Antonio whom he'd met during training in Texas. Her letters and his thoughts of her comforted him until he warmed to his new home.

In time, though, as the love letters flowed and thoughts of Dyess faded, he cozied to Germany. The beer and the cognac tasted less bitter; chasing fräuleins and brawling in the bars passed for fun; and music with his friends became like family time.

The music he played was gospel and country, and, with a group of airmen that somebody dubbed the Landsberg Barbarians, Cash delighted in belting out old standards by Ernest Tubb, Jimmie Rodgers, and Roy Acuff. *What a beautiful thought I am thinking/Concerning the great speckled bird/Remember her name is recorded/On the pages of God's Holy Word*. Content initially just to sing along, Cash soon bought a guitar and, later, a tape recorder. "It was a pretty fascinating piece of equipment," said Cash of the machine, "and central to the creative life of the Landsberg Barbarians...."

We'd sit around together in the barracks and murder the country songs of the day and the gospel songs of our youth—we were all country boys, so we all knew them—and that tape recorder would let us hear the results."

Like when he listened to his mother's hymns or glued his ear to the harmonizing Louvin Brothers on radio throughout his boyhood, a germ of musical creativity wriggled to life again in Landsberg. He turned the three chords he knew inside and out, and plied his songwriting, penning a number of tunes, including "Hey Porter," "Run Softly Blue River," and "Oh What a Dream," all of which he later recorded professionally. The air force proved to be Cash's Juilliard, a place of formation—musically and emotionally.

As crucial particles of Cash's musical development gathered in Landsberg, the seeds of the *Johnny Cash At Folsom Prison* album were being sown. Cash first learned of Folsom Prison in 1953, two years into his air force hitch, when he saw Crane Wilbur's film *Inside the Walls of Folsom Prison*. The 90-minute feature, which has long since dissolved into obscurity, starred Steve Cochran as a crusading prisoner battling a tyrannical warden (and featured in a bit part budding actor and singer Sheb Wooley, who many years later made his home near Cash in Hendersonville, Tennessee). The movie was pure B grade, maligned in the press for its formulaic plot and destined for a fleeting run in the nation's cinemas. *The Washington Post* dismissed it: "The new picture gets mighty wrought up about sadistic prison officials, lingers long over violence, reaches its most exciting peak with an attempted prison break and winds up by stating that all this was a long while ago and if not the millennium, at least wisdom has come to Folsom."

But what would have Cash cared for such reviews? Still a young (and entertainment-starved) man with only a vague conception of life, much less prison life, Cash responded to the movie like the creative soul he was: he wrote a song. "It was a violent movie," remembered Cash, "and I just wanted to write a song that would tell what I thought it would be like in prison."

Inside the Walls of Folsom Prison earned a legacy when it inspired Cash to write a song. However, as cinematography, art, or story-telling, the film disintegrated. Echoing *The Washington Post* in 1951, *The New York Times* review suggests that *Inside the Walls* was doomed from the start:

"Warner Brothers, those inveterate cinema penologists, are 'in stir' again, and the old place, which never was grimmer, is still the same. This time they are studying Folsom, one of California's noted gaols, in 'Inside the Walls of Folsom Prison,' which came to the Globe on Saturday. And, though Bryan Foy the producer, who obviously is in favor of reform, pokes his cameras into dark cell blocks, towers, yards and rock quarries of the penitentiary, all he captures is another prison picture indistinguishable from those uninspired melodramas that have come regularly from the West."

Stills from the Warner Bros. film Inside the Walls of Folsom Prison. (Courtesy of the author's collection)

The young poet's work empathized with the prisoner's life as much as a military man or a lonely lover could, dwelling on the frustration of freedom denied. Although the line *I shot a man in Reno/Just to watch him die* remains the song's most memorable and often raised yelps, grins, and chuckles among his audiences, the complexity of the song is not in its violence or even its repentance (two qualities so linked to Cash's image today), but rather in its loneliness and longing for the right to once again move about without shackles. *I know I had it comin'/I know I can't be free/But those people keep a-movin'/And that's what tortures me.*

One might gather from the song that Cash had marked time in a cell block, but he only had an idea of such existence based on Hollywood dramatics, solitude in Landsberg, and the tragic death of his brother Jack, which in his childhood had made him a prisoner of guilt and grief. So many of us live like prisoners, he said years later: "I think prison songs are popular because most of us are living in one little kind of prison or another, and whether we know it or not the words of a song about someone who is actually in a prison speak for a lot of us who might appear not to be, but really are."

One might also gather from the lines of "Folsom" that Cash had shown fast maturation as a song writer, bottling in one blow grief, loneliness, violence, regret, along with the Western imagery of lawlessness and dark trains hurtling across the horizon. It seemed to be a thoroughly legitimate heir to the country music themes of tragedy and heartbreak that fathers and mothers such as Jimmie Rodgers, the Carter Family, and Vernon Dalhart had so convincingly revealed to earlier generations. But far from it. Although Cash innocently borrowed *I shot a man in Reno/Just to watch him die* from Rodgers' "Blue Yodel No. 1 (T for Texas)", which contained the equally harrowing *I'm gonna shoot poor Thelma/Just to see her jump and fall,* the genes of "Folsom Prison Blues" dwelled in an unlikely parent: a 1953 album cut written by arranger and conductor Gordon Jenkins, whose best-known work came later in collaboration with Frank Sinatra. Cash brazenly lifted the skeleton and much of the flesh from Jenkins' "Crescent City Blues," which appeared on his experimental concept album *Seven Dreams*.

Seven Dreams, the 1953 LP by Gordon Jenkins and source of "Folsom Prison Blues."

As Cash's 1955 recording of "Folsom Prison Blues" revealed, Cash adapted "Crescent City's" tune (a traditional blues that Jenkins could not claim as his own), and plagiarized large chunks of the lyrics. Although he didn't copy all of "Crescent City Blues" word for word, the songs' similarities are so close that one wonders why Cash made so little effort to disguise his deed, particularly when he wrote his fourth stanza, the first two lines of which virtually mirror the following lines from Jenkins' composition: *If I owned that lonesome whistle/If that railroad train were mine/I'd bet I'd find a man/A little farther down the line*.

In the early 1970s—only after "Folsom Prison Blues" appeared on the *At Folsom* album—Jenkins extracted a hefty payment from Cash.

If "Folsom Prison Blues" had grown from Cash alone, only the Jimmie Rodgers' line borrowed, one might conclude that the composition was enormously promising from a songwriting standpoint, but Cash would have to prove himself as a songwriter elsewhere. Even in adapting Jenkins' lyrics, he exposed his flaws: The inchoate lyricist either forgot or confused his geography, placing the man who'd murdered in Nevada behind bars in a California state prison and meditating on a train running down to San Antone, a destination for no train passing Folsom (not without a year of station stops, anyway). Perhaps Cash placed Folsom in Texas or in Nevada? It's hard to know: When Cash spoke publicly about the song in later years, he focused primarily on the *Reno* line. Whatever the roots of Cash's plagiarism and confusion, the passing years have absolved him. Unlike its main character who withers behind bars, "Folsom Prison Blues" transcended its ignoble birth.

Just weeks after mustering out of the air force at Camp Kilmer, New Jersey, Cash married Vivian Liberto on August 7, 1954. Gravitating to his family in the mid-South, Cash and his Texas bride settled in Memphis, where they rented a small apartment and immediately started on a family of their own. While Vivian kept house, J.R. crisscrossed the streets of Memphis selling used appliances and in spare hours attended radio broadcasting school. But an agitation borne of air force tedium and selling for selling's sake crept up his back: "I really couldn't get my mind on anything but music," wrote Cash. "I spent more time in my car listening to the radio than I did knocking on doors. At night, I'd lay awake listening to the record shows."

Whenever he could, he performed his air force songs for family and friends, and joined two mechanics, Luther Perkins and Marshall Grant—both of whom he'd met through his brother Roy—for regular jam sessions. The practicing continued "night after night," recalled Cash, "just for the love of it." Re-creating nights in the barracks with the Landsberg Barbarians, the three (Grant on bass and Perkins on the bass strings of the electric guitar) plowed through country standards, gospel favorites, and Cash's own tunes, musing all the while about the places music could take them. By and by, they landed a spate of local gigs, and showed up a few times on radio across the Mississippi River in West Memphis, Arkansas. Stepping forward in late 1954, Cash lurched toward a recording career, dialing up Sam Phillips of Sun Records, who was busy at the time minting Elvis

Presley's eternal discs. The wiry air force vet attired himself in gospel uniform for Phillips, but Elvis Presley's new mentor replied that gospel belonged in the church, not in the catalog of a small record company trying to make money. "There's something different about you guys," admitted Phillips. "But I can't use gospel stuff. You come up with something else and come back."

Undaunted, Cash and the guys soon returned to Phillips' Memphis Recording Service on 706 Union Avenue with a satchel of devil's music that moved Phillips to set up a recording date. On March 22, 1955—with Vivian barely two months away from delivering their first child, Rosanne Cash— J.R. and his band (which included that day a steel guitarist named Red Kernodle) tumbled into the studio, and stumbled through five songs, including "Hey Porter," which Phillips pressed on to Cash's first single later in the year.

"Hey Porter," which the band had tirelessly rehearsed in Marshall Grant's home, was immediately startling, a commanding voice calling to the man in front of the train car: *When we hit Dixie would you tell the engineer to ring his bell/And tell everybody that ain't asleep to stand right up and yell*. The lyric was as bold as the voice was startling, a proud Southern boast unrivaled until Lynard Skynard came up with "Sweet Home Alabama" in 1974. Throughout Cash's keep-your-North vocals, Marshall and Luther churned out a complementing train rhythm, which would become their trademark boom-chicka-boom sound, but the session lost its steam when Phillips and the band turned for the first time to "Folsom Prison Blues." Tackling the song in a fit of bi-polar mania, Cash wavered between a ghastly high-pitched Elvis imitation and his natural bass baritone, while Luther's fingers wandered like scared ducks through a halting electric guitar solo. Nothing but "Hey Porter" was salvageable from the day's work.

Cash with the Tennessee Two in the 1950s on WSM's Grand Ole Opry, Marshall Grant (left) and Luther Perkins (center). (Courtesy of Bear Family Records)

The Tennessee Two share the plight of the Blue Moon Boys...well, two of the Blue Moon Boys. Like Scotty Moore and Bill Black who thrust their vocalist into fame with their ecstatic instrumentation only to recede behind his phenomenal star power, Marshall Grant and Luther Perkins helped create a sound that became solely identified with Johnny Cash. Injustice? Perhaps. But in the marketing of music, charisma trumps shared credit every time. Elvis and Johnny rode up front on the sounds they had created with other men.

If Luther and Marshall groused about their supporting role in the Johnny Cash story, their discontent never rose above the telling of the Cash tale. Two mechanics, Perkins and Grant met Cash in 1954 and remained in tight musical collaboration until August of 1968—a few months after the Folsom concert—when Perkins died from injuries sustained in a house fire. (Grant remained with Cash into the 1980s.)

Over the years, whether performing a Bob Dylan ballad or an A. P. Carter standard, Cash's sound rarely strayed from the loping rhythm that the three had created in Memphis. The bobbing boom-chicka-boom may have turned away those who thought it monotonous, but others found it startling, a jarring invitation to the music, or familiar like the steady rumble of a trusty automobile. "The...instrumental style suited me, and it came naturally to us," said Cash. "Marshall Grant was mostly right when in later years he said that we didn't work to get that boom-chicka-boom sound—it's all we could play. But it served us well, and it was ours. You knew whose voice was coming when you heard it kick off."

The sound that heralded Johnny Cash was pounded out in the basement of Marshall Grant's home at 4199 Nakomis Avenue in east Memphis. There, they first jammed on acoustic guitars until Luther showed up with a little Fender Telecaster out of Sid Lapworth's music shop. Lapworth, Perkins told Marshall, also had a "big doghouse upright bass" sitting around. "You oughta go up and talk to him about it." A few nights later, Grant—who'd never played a bass—lugged in the used instrument from Lapworth's and introduced it to Cash's acoustic guitar and Perkins' electric.

Early promotional portrait.
(Courtesy of Bear Family Records)

It was an uneasy marriage. Grant taped little bits of paper to the bass to help him find the notes; Cash struggled to keep up a rhythm on his guitar; and Perkins labored to control his volume. "He couldn't turn it down enough with the amplifier," explains Grant. So Luther coped by muffling the open strings with his hand, while picking out a rhythm on the bass strings. Agreeing to try something in E, much as newlyweds might randomly decide on a brand of coffee to buy, they pressed forward behind the tip-tap, tip-tap of Luther's halting rhythm. "John joined in, and I started playing bass," says Grant. "And the first time I ever hit the string, I started slapping it. For whatever reason, I don't know. Moral of the story is [that in] eight bars, and only eight bars, the sound of Johnny Cash was created right then and there. Yes, we were all very, very, very limited. And as we got along a little bit ... I remember very, very well the 21st time that I ever played the bass with John and Luther ... we recorded 'Hey Porter.' And that sound ... is what Sam [Phillips] heard. And not only the three instruments, but John's voice blended with it so well. It's just something that God put on this earth for us to do."

One futilely rakes the mind to name a more identifiable instrumental sound in the spectrum of popular music. Walk by a group of people and hum Luther's familiar bass notes, and the reaction is "Johnny Cash"; the lyrics to "I Walk the Line" or "Folsom Prison Blues" may elude them, but pulsing from within—as organic as a heartbeat—is the boom-chicka-boom.

On July 30, 1955, they revisited "Folsom," this time with a finely tuned arrangement. In the glow of Phillips' warm slapback echo, which Phillips conjured by looping sound back through his recording console, Cash glided through the grim lyric like a harrow through soft, pebbly earth, while the Tennessee Two guardedly pumped out the rhythm. It may be the quintessential Cash recording: brooding, sparse, anchored by boom-chicka-boom, in the voice of those leagues below society's radar, and distinguished by the unflappable Luther Perkins' licks. Sun Records scholar Hank Davis held that the electric guitarist may have turned in the performance of his life on "Folsom": "His solo … is one of the few times Luther ventured off the bass strings. It remains totally memorable and, in the ultimate gesture of respect, is often repeated note for note by technically superior musicians." When Luther forgot his bashfulness and stretched for the higher range, he became the second voice on the recording. Far more than guitar acrobatics, his licks were pulsing tears, hypnotic days in prison. All at once, the team had nailed the sound of prison's monotony, and perfected the pitch of Cash's blasted passing train.

(left) The sheet music of "Folsom Prison Blues." (right) The original 45 rpm single of "Folsom Prison Blues" on Sun, released in 1955.

Folsom Prison Blues

Words and Music by
JOHNNY CASH

Moderately (not too slow)

mf

CHORUS

G

1. I   hear the train a - com - in';   it's   roll - in' 'round the   bend,   And
2. When I   was just a   ba - by   my   ma - ma told   me,   "Son, _____

Hi Lo Music
BMI
232

FOLSOM PRISON BLUES
(Cash)
JOHNNY CASH
and the
TENNESSEE TWO
MEMPHIS, TENNESSEE

Those people keep a' movin'/And that's what tortures me.

In December, Phillips released "Folsom Prison Blues" backed with "So Doggone Lonesome." In February, "Folsom" reached number four on the country charts and bored into the core of Johnny Cash's repertoire.

In the glow of "Folsom" and other gems of the 1950s such as "I Walk the Line" and "Home of the Blues," Cash molded a recorded legacy that was anything but country conventional, despite his sustained and lofty presence on the genre's popularity charts. The unrelenting boom-chicka-boom rhythm may have suggested to some rut and uniformity, but his catalog explored Zeus's realm. At Sun, he stuck to his dark ballad jag, but he also went straight country and western, and swung for the kids in the Elvis Presley corps with his "Ballad of a Teenage Queen" and "Guess Things Happen That Way." And when he left Sun and signed with Columbia Records in 1958, he proved no less experimental, taking control of his recordings despite the presence of legendary producer Don Law and his co-producer Frank Jones. Law and Jones could only stand by as Cash cussedly set to wax his beloved hymns, tributes to his country influences, and bold classics such as "Ring of Fire" and "I Got Stripes." "John had his own way," says Jones.

Critics and industry suits who draped Cash in country ignored the true expanse of his endeavors. Cash had effectively submerged only one foot in

On the road: (left to right) unidentified, Cash, Porter Wagoner, Hawkshaw Hawkins, unidentified.
(Courtesy of the author's collection)

country music since the beginning of his recording career, rolling on to the American scene in the rock and roll company of Elvis Presley, Jerry Lee Lewis, Carl Perkins, and the rest of the Sun Records team. Even as country music, his 1950s recordings were just barely: they strutted rock and roll style and ached like cracked, dry skin, far scalier than the Nashville Sound that was melting over country music and rougher too than the jingling honky-tonk styles of Porter Wagoner and Ray Price, two men who kept the Nashville Sound at arm's length in the 1950s. "I never did like musical bags, you know?" Cash told *Rolling Stone* in 1992. "We busted out on our own at Sun Records in the Fifties, with our long hair and sideburns and black clothes, and they called us every name under the sun, from 'rockabilly' to 'white nigger.' I took it with pride, because they were telling me, 'You're different.' I didn't set out to sound different from everybody else, but when I realized that I *was* different, then I was thrilled to death."

Delighting in his difference, Cash proved an uneasy guest in the country music house, shirking the control of producers and refusing to settle his family in Nashville, moving instead to the suburbs of Los Angeles. He despised country music's venerated hub, the *Grand Ole Opry,* for the blinders on its bridle and forsook its city, despite the general belief that no singer with a country audience could thrive elsewhere. His outright distaste for Nashville—which should be distinguished from his love for individual Nashville-based performers of the day such as Hank Snow and Ernest Tubb—drew blood in 1965 when he smashed a line of footlights on the *Grand Ole Opry* stage. Drugs and frustration conspired in the frightening outburst, but the act symbolized Cash's feelings for country music's establishment.

Backstage in the early 1960s.
(Courtesy of the author's collection)

Snubbing that establishment, he conspicuously adored the early minstrels of hillbilly cum country music, turning to the current folk scene, which plainly valued those seminal figures more than Nashville did. To invigorate the country music tradition, Cash endeavored to—believed he'd been ordained to—pull together a new library of American folk music. "I'm trying to sell authentic folk music," he told *Time* in 1959. In the ballads he wrote or adapted, he remembered the lives of almost every imaginable laborer: the cotton picker, the gravedigger, the roughneck, the coal miner, the train engineer, the lumberjack, the spike driver. And he painted the power and beauty of nature in "Five Feet High and Rising" (1959), "Forty Shades of Green" (1961), and "You Wild Colorado" (1964). When he didn't write his own songs or adapt them from some ancient ode or melody, he tapped those who were creating or had created modern folk music, writers such as Merle Travis, Peter La Farge, and June Carter, whom he had hired for his road show in the early 1960s and would marry in 1968 after he and Vivian divorced.

Considering his musical interests, it should have surprised nobody in the mid-1960s when Cash sought out Bob Dylan, the most innovative figure in popular music since Elvis. To many, Cash's friendship with Dylan must have seemed as unlikely as the Kennedy-Johnson ticket, but Cash had always sought unlikely stimulation from outside his walls, soaking up blues in black Memphis and permitting Presley's rockabilly and Sister Rosetta Tharpe's gospel to permeate him. "He was chameleon-like," observes Harold Reid of the Statler Brothers, who worked with Cash for many years starting in the early 1960s. "He would soak up whatever he was around and found a way to use it then to his advantage." Dylan pricked his ear.

Promotional portrait of Cash and June Carter.
(Courtesy of the author's collection)

Cash discovered Dylan when Columbia's venerated executive John Hammond gave him the talkin' blues-filled *Freewheelin' Bob Dylan* LP in 1963. Convinced that Dylan's piercing voice and cutting verse was that of a Mississippi songwriter, Cash was knocked out, and he immediately wrote a fan letter to the lad, initiating a correspondence that lasted through the decade. In Dylan, Cash saw a comrade, a worshipper of early musical traditions, and a new voice apart from the bland pop music of the day.

As the years passed, the first public meeting between Cash and Dylan became a mythical summit of the gods, when it was really merely the handshake of two men seeking their musical destinies: Cash yearning to peel off the labels of country music and Dylan in the midst of shedding his protest cloak. They met at the Newport Folk Festival in the summer of 1964.

The folk gathering in Rhode Island had been the summit for folk enthusiasts around the country since 1959, a highly attended event that showcased the talents of a new generation of folk voices and re-introduced olden voices from bluegrass, the blues, and the ballad traditions. Cash—this self-styled singer of folk songs—must have swooned in the hub of Newport's folk activity when he showed up there, for it implicitly affirmed his earthen songwriting in a way unimaginable on country radio or on the *Grand Ole Opry* (from which he'd be soon banished following the footlights episode).

Few mainstream country artists had ever rated among Newport organizers, but Cash's folk credentials had recently begun to harden in the eyes of coffee house and college crowds who sojourned every year to the worn-on-the-corners old money town in Rhode Island. In March of 1964, those crowds had seen him in the pages of the *Broadside* folk sheet, railing in verse against Bob Dylan's second guessers who picked through the minstrel's piercing lyrics like rag women scouring a dump. *I got hung, but didn't choke ... /Bob Dylan slung his rope/ ... Don't bad mouth him, till you hear him/Let him start by continuing/He's almost brand new/SHUT UP! ... AND LET HIM SING!*

Then on the eve of Newport, in the wake of his *Broadside* diatribe, Cash released Greenwich Village denizen Peter La Farge's "Ballad of Ira Hayes," a plaintive testament to hopelessness among American Indians that Columbia-Nashville staffer Gene Ferguson had introduced to him earlier in the year. *Call him drunkin' Ira Hayes/He won't answer anymore/Not the whiskey drinkin' Indian/Or the Marine who went to war.* With a voice that seemed to come right out of the ditch where Hayes breathed his last, Cash solidified his status in the land of the folk, an achievement which would serve him in 1968 when sections of the folk audience helped create a frenzy around *Johnny Cash At Folsom Prison.*

Still, as he anticipated Newport, one might have expected him to be little more comfortable with the festival than he was on a Nashville stage, filled with schoolboy trepidation, unsure if the crowd would accept him and nervous about meeting Dylan and his girlfriend Joan Baez. But it appeared not. A day tardy, having missed his scheduled slot the day before, he swaggered on stage yelping and dishing out his usual stage patter: "Is there any water here?... I got some water last time I was here.... I don't know what it run off of." He cobbled out the best he had to offer for Newport: his neo-folk standards "Big River" and "Folsom Prison Blues," peppered with La

Farge's "Ira Hayes," Dylan's "Don't Think Twice It's Alright," and A. P. Carter's "Keep on the Sunnyside."

Regal in his jet black suit and white-ruffled dress shirt, Cash dashed backstage after his victorious set, into the arms of Dylan. A photographer posed them, stubble-faced country star with his arm draped around his little musical brother. Cash played the giddy teenager showing off his new pair of Cuban-heeled boots. Dylan, as folk singer Eric Anderson witnessed, danced in delight: "I was backstage, and Bob ran over and grabbed me. 'You've gotta meet Johnny Cash man!' Cash was a hero to us, one of the original cats. So Bob brought me back to his tent, and I met John. He had just done his set, and he was really wired. He looked like a puppet whose strings were all tangled up—half cut and half held together—and he was just jiggling around." A night of informal guitar pulling followed, according to Robert Shelton in his 1986 biography of Dylan:

> Cash was hustled off to Baez's room at the Viking Motor Inn, where he and Dylan taped some songs for her. Cash, whose craggy, granite-hewn exterior made him look tough all the way through, was deeply touched by his acceptance. He had been a big country star and then his emotions and hard living had nearly done him in. He was beginning that long march toward stardom again, and he was filled with fears.... To find Newport so warm made him feel even taller than he was. It touched him to find that the two young stars of the folk world, Baez and Dylan, cared enough about him to spend the whole night taping him. To show his appreciation, he gave Dylan one of his own guitars. The next morning, Baez talked proudly of the evening.

In rumbling through "Don't Think Twice" at Newport, Cash had embodied the crossroads where traditional country music and modern folk music met. Writing in the *New York Times*, Shelton said the Memphis boy was "closing the gap between Nashville and Newport." And when news spread of Cash and Dylan hanging out backstage and around town, the crossroads merged into one road. The meeting at Newport also represented a bend in the road for both men: Dylan would presently embark down a country road that culminated in the *Nashville Skyline* LP of 1969, and Cash left town quenched with the belief that his music was indeed universal.

Not long after Newport, while parked in Manhattan for a while, Cash and a few of his troupe loaded into taxis and rode to Greenwich Village, searching for the Gaslight on MacDougal Street, a spot tucked in the neighborhood's labyrinth of streets. When Cash paced down the steps into the coffee house, Peter La Farge recalled a skeptical buzz about the room. "What's he doing here?" "What does he want?" He sat awhile before a guitar appeared, and then settling on stage, he shifted around, caressed the strings, and drifted into "I Walk the Line." Don and Harold Reid, who were along that night, saw Cash recapture the potency of the very first recording, now almost ten years old. "Everything that Luther did, John did it on a flattop guitar, and we had never seen him or heard him do that before," says Harold Reid. The wary crowd burst with acceptance. Documented in the pages of the folk journal *Sing Out!*, it was another small triumph in his courting of the folk audience.

"He could turn on to whatever particular audience that he wanted," adds Don Reid. "He did that night. He could read 'em quick."

When Cash linked his name with Dylan's, he not only bought entrée to the folk and rock worlds, he gained respect among music journalists who generally crinkled their noses at country. Robert Shelton, who never needed a tutorial in country music, had become a big fan, spotlighting Cash whenever he appeared in the Big Apple, and a *Time* critic allowed that he was "the best of the modern country singer-composers." Even *Sing Out!*, the mouthpiece of the folk music movement, bowed to him, dubbing him a "great American voice."

However, most journalists who condescended to point their pens toward Nashville had eyes that only saw an urban cow pie, writing about the town and its music with nastiness and patronization. In the national press's view, Nashville was a Bible-thumping, blue law–blighted backwater, its performers comic-page characters, or as *Time* sneered in 1964, "back-hill singers and strummers, sporting mail-order toupees and $300 hand-tooled boots."

Harper's Larry L. King—a Texan who should have known better—killed a night at the *Grand Ole Opry,* while longing all the while, it seemed, for his room service and thousand-fingers massage: "The Opry House—the Ryman Auditorium—is an old red-brick eyesore with balconies and church-like windows, and without air conditioning." Jazz critic Gene Lees called Nashville a "pallid, tasteless town" before wearing down his *High Fidelity* readers with a perfunctory visit to a few Music Row offices. This was the same Lees who—once settled convivially back in New York splendor— called the instrumentation of veteran Nashville pickers "semi-literate tonic dominant strummings of itinerants."

Such treatment in the press threatened to sully Cash, but he managed to dodge most of the flying dirt. Lees referred to his "singular quality of realism," but such compliments lay buried in articles that dwelled on Nudie suits and Webb Pierce's geetar-shaped swimming pool. Gaining respectability in the mainstream press was tough for a country boy. But Cash's friendship with Dylan had helped. And when journalists spotted the flames from the house-on-fire sales of *At Folsom* in 1968, they were poised to fan them with generous, even fawning, language.

Cash's exploration of the folk scene invigorated his music—he was like a child splashing in a new rubber pool—but his personal and professional worlds were as tenuous as his music was refreshed. A dark, imprisoned side of Cash, induced by drugs and frustrations personal and professional, threatened to take down his music and his well-being. Since the late 1950s, speed had been a regular course in his diet, and his highs and search for more highs, as time went by, emaciated his body and warped his moods. In the professional realm, says producer Frank Jones, he would often arrive late and unprepared for sessions, then saunter over to his guitar, tickle it, and go home: "There were times we were very worried about him.... He would be involved in his habit, and ... it got pretty bad at times. And there wasn't anything we could do to try to get him to see doctors or something...."

We just didn't record, just let him go and come back when he was feeling better. That's all we could do."

But sessions weren't always that way. Ironically, in the early to mid-1960s, as his drug use escalated, he recorded some of the finest performances of his career. This was an era of hit singles, and layered below them was a trilogy of concept albums that may still be the most important albums ever made by a country artist: *Ride This Train* (1960), *Blood, Sweat and Tears* (1963), and *Bitter Tears* (1964). Each was recorded with varying amounts of chemicals running through his blood, yet each was innovative in country music, dedicating album-length attention to the legacy of the westward expansion, the working man, and the American Indian, respectively. And although other country artists had certainly recorded concept albums and honored Indians and laborers before Cash, none had committed three albums to the topics, and no one appeared to treat such topics as seriously as Johnny Cash. "I got a lot of credit for it among the other artists," Cash told Robert Hilburn. "A lot of other people openly admired them, but some people didn't want to accept the fact that a country artist was doing things like that. I had a few people tell me that it wasn't country and that it wasn't right for me to do it. They said it wasn't commercial and all that jazz." Commercial or not, Cash continued, recording another ramble through the West, *Johnny Cash Sings Ballads of the True West* in 1966, and religiously weaving into his songs and repertoire the downtrodden and the common man.

However, when he failed to transcend the drugs' mire, the sound could be hard on the ear. An album of novelties, *Everybody Loves a Nut* (1966), was ill-conceived at best, and through many performances, his voice was hoarse, raw, as if he were battling a cold. Listen to his gasping, cracking vocals on *Ballads of the True West*. "I got to where I had chronic laryngitis because I kept myself so dried out. And my voice would go and stay gone. I'd feel sorry for myself, and I'd go off and hide somewhere."

The drug use dogged his live performances as well. Peppered among his many brilliant shows (which included Carl Perkins, the Statler Brothers, the Carter Family—featuring June, Helen, Anita, and Mother Maybelle—all for three bucks!) were pitiful, unreal nights when Marshall Grant all but pushed him on the stage as Cash dangled between consciousness and unconsciousness. Fits of giggling beset him. He slurred his lyrics. He forgot the words. A 1962 performance at Carnegie Hall, which should have been a showcase to expand his audience, crashed horribly. On a bill with the Glaser Brothers, Mac Wiseman, and George Jones, Cash meant to pay homage to Jimmie Rodgers in his segment of the show, but only a few ragged notes croaked out. The triumph of Newport still two years in his future, *New York Times* critic Robert Shelton lambasted him: "He is known as a song-writer and singer in the vein of some of the country greats, such as the late Jimmie Rodgers and the late Hank Williams. But the hoarseness of his voice and the incohesiveness of his performance suggest that another hearing is needed before his name can be mentioned in the company of such reputable country minstrels."

Cash never earned such a lousy review again in New York, but the embarrassment failed to deter him from his speed-forged road. As the 1960s wore on, his erraticism accelerated as he missed shows or flubbed them. In one of his last fits of irresponsibility, he skipped three shows at a county fair in Arthur, Illinois, and for thanks felt the slap of a lawsuit. "There was several shows during that period there when we couldn't find him for three or four days," said Marshall Grant. "Maybe in the middle of the afternoon he'd go to bed, or pass out. Sometimes it wasn't even in bed. And no matter what we had to do that night, didn't matter, if we had to cancel a show or whatever, we would not wake him up. Because if you let him sleep it off, you could probably make the rest of the tour. If you woke him up, pretty good chance that you weren't. We probably wasn't making 50 percent of the engagements at that time…. A lot of them, we simply couldn't find him. So, you know, you just have to understand him and go accordingly."

The payment for another binge around the time of the Arthur, Illinois, events was something close to death. Cash's first biographer, Christopher Wren, placed the scene in Toronto, in the fall of 1966. After a show and a ritual feast of amphetamines, Cash disappeared in the rain-soaked city. At 3:00 A.M., Marshall Grant found him at an after-hours club and attempted to lure him away by telling him his daughter Rosanne was sick. Cash promised to come soon. "He showed up about daylight," recalls Grant. "And they called me, woke me up. I had been in bed about an hour or so. I told him, 'John, you know there's nothing wrong with Rosanne. She's fine. I just had to tell you something to get you back over here to sleep because we've got a matinee show tomorrow in Watertown, New York." The bass player cajoled Cash into getting some sleep before the bus pulled out later in the morning.

"At 7:00 I went to his room, I always kept a key to his room, and he wasn't there. And it was a mess. His clothes were scattered everywhere. Just a horrible mess. I put all of his clothes in his bag and took 'em downstairs and started looking for him. I asked the bellboy and he said, 'Well, I saw him come in, but I don't know where he went.'" Grant dashed to the motor home they traveled in, and found the door locked from the inside. "I knew he was in there, couldn't see in there 'cause he had all the curtains pulled. So I got a little side pouch along side the bus that I carried a few tools in ... and I took that side window out right at the driver. And I finally got in the bus through that window right there, and when I go in there ... he was settin' on the couch across from the dinette and he had passed out, and his head went down on the floor but his butt was still up on the seat. And he had a knife in his hand. I could see the handle of the knife and I thought he stuck it in his throat or somethin' but I didn't see no blood."

Cash had been peeling and eating potatoes and onions when he passed out, and his mouth was stuffed with them. His breathing had stopped. "I raked all the stuff out of his mouth the best I could, and I started blowin' air in his lungs, and I pushed on his stomach like I saw people do on TV. That was all I know. And I got hysterical with it. I pushed and I'd blow and I'd push and I'd blow, and this went on for about five minutes.... But directly I heard him grunt, and so I did it some more. And I kept on and I could see a faint breath. Then I know that it went on for about 15 minutes. Then I saw one of his eyes open just a little bit. Just one of them."

Marshall Grant in 1968.
(Photo by Jim Marshall)

Grant rushed into the hotel restaurant for help, and with one of the band members, he hoisted the motionless Cash onto his bed and continued to work him until his breathing returned to normal. It was almost business as usual, just one of many such frantic episodes. Marshall revved up the motor home with New York in mind, knowing all along, though, that they'd meet a thorough inspection by border guards who knew that where there are entertainers there are drugs—and addicts. As they approached the United States, Marshall and June buried Cash under a small mound of speakers, instruments and blankets, hoping that the guards would miss him. They did.

The Johnny Cash show arrived in Watertown just as the show was beginning. Grant remembers that Faron Young had just taken the stage. Cash, however, was still deep in a stupor. Somebody raided the concession stand and began plying the singer with coffee and juice. "June and I worked feverishly on him, and we got him to stand up," says Grant. "He could stand up. And he could hear us. I said, 'John, let me tell you, we're in Watertown, New York. We're at the concert. Faron Young is gettin' ready to come off, we got so-and-so goin' on the stage, then we're gonna take a little intermission and you're gonna go on stage.' And he didn't say nothing, and he sat back down. I said, 'John, I'm gonna tell you, you gotta go on stage now. You gotta cooperate and you gotta get your act together because we're here, the building's full and you've got to go on stage.'"

Cash's band, with Grant, walked on stage and dove into an opening number, not knowing if Cash would take his cue. Cash took it, and he finished an abbreviated show.

"Nobody knew there was anything wrong with him," recalls Grant. "He had that ability." In the year after this drama, Cash proved that he also had the ability to at least partially subdue his drug problem.

Over the years, writers, including Cash, have portrayed Cash's emergence from drugs as an overnight conversion that occurred in 1967.

The stories vary: Cash spends night in Georgia jail, receives scolding from the sheriff, and heads home determined to go clean, or Cash hikes deep into Nickajack Cave, resolved to just die there, but hears a voice urging him to persevere. According to the story, Cash marries June Carter, gets right with God, and rides happily into the 1970s.

But Cash's turn in the battle with drug addiction is not so easily pin-pointed. The moments in the jail and in the cave may have cracked open the door, but they ultimately were small steps in a protracted and difficult journey to a less intense addiction. The journey, though, had begun in 1967, after his missed shows in Illinois, the spelunking excursion into Nickajack Cave, and a bizarre observance of his late brother Jack's birthday, for which he invited all of his family but was too high to host them. Looking at his challenge very biblically, Cash told Robert Hilburn that he had felt change coming. "I'd had seven years of roughing it and I felt I had seven years of good times and good life coming. I really felt in 1967 that there were seven big years ahead."

With the support of June Carter and Tennessee psychologist Nat Winston, Cash set out on a bumpy path. He pledged abstinence during recovery, but sneaked pills behind the backs of his caretakers. Cravings gnawed at him. Sometimes he succumbed to them; sometimes he brushed them away. It was a battle of attrition, two strides forward then back again. However, flying in the face of many doubters he had ratcheted down his dependence by the tail end of 1967: the pills still regularly seduced him, but his manic appetite for them had abated by degrees. As he had envisioned, a period of prosperity rose in front of him.

Cash spent the latter half of '67 on the road, stopping by the recording studio for two days only; in early October, he waxed three songs, two of which comprised a single for release in November. Cash had never stayed away from the studio for so long, which suggests that when he wasn't on stage, he was at home wrestling down the drugs. Or in jail wrestling down the drugs ... or in a cave.

You're starting fresh. We don't even care what you've done. You act like a man here, we treat you like a man. You get stupid with us, we get stupid back. And if you don't understand what that means, that means if you want to start fighting with us, then we're going to start fighting back with you. And we'll kick your ass.
— Folsom Prison guard to newly-arrived Folsom inmates

0002

Although Jimmie Rodgers uttered grizzly murder ballads in the 1920s and dozens of others had before and after him, very few artists of Cash's stature recorded hit songs in the 1950s with lyrics as brazenly violent as *I shot a man in Reno/Just to watch him die*. Nor did any artist sound as if he or she could have pulled off the bloody deed. The Kingston Trio won a country and western Grammy in 1958 for "Tom Dooley," yet few could imagine the well-scrubbed young men arriving late for dinner, much less stabbing "her with my knife"; and the honey-voiced Jim Reeves scored a hit with the treacherous "Partners" in 1959, but Gentleman Jim was the song's Voice of God narrator, well distanced from the gory scene in a miner's cabin. Cash's gallows baritone, though, suggested that its owner just might gun down a man—even worse, a woman—and enjoy watching him—or her—squirm.

"Folsom's" homicidal line and its interpreter's sawed-off shotgun delivery birthed a half century of myth, convincing many Americans that the rangy, dark-eyed man from Arkansas had done hard time for shooting a man when he had merely stewed in jail a few nights after alcohol and pill binges. But the myth endured. His audiences clung to it and over the years, Cash came to realize that trading on the myth—his tight association with the criminal world—stirred his audience's imaginations and pocket books. Nobody bought the myth more willingly than prisoners. "After 'Folsom Prison Blues,' the prisoners felt kinda like I was one of them," said Cash. "I'd get letters from them, some asking for me to come and play."

Cash and the Tennessee Two first responded to a striped invitation in 1957, agreeing to play Huntsville State Prison in Texas. At the time, nobody with a top ten hit even considered performing inside prison walls, much less reading a prisoner's letter. But Cash went ahead with the pioneering show, and although nobody remembers any fanfare around the date, they do remember a soggy day, a makeshift stage, shorted electric guitar and amps, Johnny picking and singing with no mic and no Luther, and dozens of happy, happy men. "By doing a prison concert, we were letting inmates know that somewhere out there in the free world was somebody who cared for them as human beings," said Cash, years later.

From Huntsville, Cash courted a long-standing relationship with San Quentin State Prison, California's oldest and one of its most notorious. When Cash first brought his show to San Quentin on a New Year's Day in the late '50s, a young man in the crowd convicted for a botched robbery attempt glimpsed his own future. Merle Haggard, who'd been sent up in 1958 for a three-year ride, sat spellbound by Luther's picking and Cash's showmanship and demeanor: "He was supposed to be there to sing songs, but it seemed like it didn't matter whether he was able to sing or not. He was just mesmerizing." The day inspired Haggard, who would know his own extraordinary career in country music. He channeled the gift of country music tradition from Cash that day, just as Cash had inherited it from the Louvin Brothers on the WMPS radio of his childhood and Ernest Tubb and

Jimmie Rodgers and others, but Haggard's recollection of the show also illustrates what Cash was delivering en masse to the prisoners: diversion, inspiration, solidarity. "There was a connection there," continued Haggard, "an identification. This was somebody singing a song about your personal life. Even the people who weren't fans of Johnny Cash—it was a mixture of people, all races were fans by the end of the show."

Over the next ten years, Cash logged some 30 prison shows, forgoing compensation but developing a hardened anti-prison sentiment. He witnessed the ravages of prison life in his audience, read about them in letters from prisoners, and heard about them from Rev. Floyd Gressett, Cash's pastor in California, who frequently counseled imprisoned men. An image of life wasted by incarceration, now based on observation rather than a movie, took form in Cash's mind.

The inmates' plight roused an innate compassion in Cash that often led him to act on behalf of others. Time after time, throughout his life, he slowed down to offer his hand, to orphanages, to tornado victims. He often recalled a scene from Memphis where, stepping out onto Union Avenue after signing his first contract with Sam Phillips, he encountered a panhandler to whom the perennially light singer gave the last few cents in his pocket—like the widow in the book of Mark who dropped all her coins in the temple box. After gaining fame, he had supported the American Indian, performing shows to draw attention to their cause, recording the somber tale of their plight on the album *Bitter Tears,* and forcefully promoting his recording of "Ballad of Ira Hayes," which brilliantly illustrated the American Indian's plight. He constantly drew attention to the sweat and toil of anonymous blue-collar workers because back in Dyess, Cash and his family had lived sweat and toil. Young Cash also saw all around him depravity and utter poverty that far exceeded whatever struggles the Cashes encountered. While some might dismiss the world's cruelty or just fail to notice, Cash allowed it to impress him, as it did when he observed indigent, rootless neighbors like those he described to biographer Christopher Wren. "Across the road on the Stuckey plantation ... was a three-room shotgun shack. Every year, a different family would move in and ask us if they could farm part of the crops. They were in dire poverty. They'd come with rags on their backs and maybe a skillet tied on their wagon. Mostly they just walked in. We lived in the big house across the road. My daddy wouldn't let us play with their kids sometimes because they'd have lice. Once there were three brothers, all older than I was, called Big 'un, Little 'un and Cotch, and a sister named Annabelle. Annabelle tried to take me into the bushes and scared me to death. Annabelle was sixteen. I was twelve." To Wren, he described people to whom death was matter of fact: a father who buried his baby in a ditch bank, a six-year-old who poisoned his father. He digested such wretched dramas, realizing their actors deserved his pity and help. As an adult, he carried those scenes with him as if they were sacred beads, invoking Christ's golden rule as he walked with Indians, common people, and prisoners.

By and by prison reform became his grand crusade, although he blanched at the term: "I didn't go into it thinking about it as a 'crusade,'" said Cash when writer Paul Hemphill encountered him in the late 1960s. "I mean, I just don't think prisons do any good. They put 'em in there and just make 'em worse, if they were ever bad in the first place, and then when they let 'em out they're just better at whatever put 'em in there in the first place. Nothing good ever came out a prison. That's all I'm trying to say."

He realized that his name could call attention to prison issues and his shows could salve—if only fleetingly—troubled, bored prisoners. "From the very first prison I played in 1957 ... I found that a concert is a tension reliever. A prison is always full of tension, but sometimes it gets to the breaking point and there's trouble. I'm not saying that our concerts have prevented trouble, but who knows? ... That's our purpose, to give them a little relief."

In the wake of his 1968 show at Folsom Prison and the popular album that came of it, Cash's prominence on the prison reform issue ballooned. What for more than ten years had been charity work—a little tension relief for the prisoners and him—became a cause in 1968. The show, which also revived his career, anointed him as a major spokesperson on prison reform. He had the ears of governors, testified in Congress on behalf of prisoners, and continued to shine a light into prisons at home and abroad through the 1970s.

The Christian press, particularly, raised him up as a haggard prophet who envisioned for the mote-blinded churches Isaiah's dream of an age when prisoners would emerge into the day's light. "No one, least of all Johnny Cash, is advocating immediate release of all convicts," declared Southern clerics Donald G. Shockley and Richard L. Freeman. "But in the name of Him who was united with thieves in his death the churches might blend their voices with a country bard who, in one respect at least, sees Isaiah's vision somewhat more vividly than they do." When Cash died in 2003, *Christian Century* eulogized a man who wished redemption for society's hell-bound, pointing to his performance of "He Turned the Water into Wine" at San Quentin in 1969: "It takes no stretch to get to the point: If Jesus could do that with something as ordinary as water, then he can make something out of the vulgar, the lonely, the lost—all the sinners, caught or not."

Nobody, least of all Cash, probably ever suspected that the Folsom show would sling him into the vortex of prison reform where the priests, politicians, and padlocked angrily debated. If nothing else, the prospect of recording at Folsom appealed to the commercial side of Cash, to the showman who believed that his hit song and the prison from which it took its name should be united with tape rolling. The showman also knew that if the prison's inmates were suitably rowdy the whole mess could make for a fabulously electric album.

Folsom Prison sits above the American River, fulgent amid hills of waving grasses and scrubby oaks. The long approach from the road on a gently curving lane might well be the entrance to the Hamilton or Trask ranches in Steinbeck's *East of Eden,* but there is no white-washed, rooster-red farmstead to be found. Hammered into the rocks some 25 miles northeast of Sacramento, the fortress of granite stares down its suppliants. Bleached, forbidding walls climb eastward from the deep river gorge to the central prison campus only to cascade down to the prison frontage south of the main buildings. Guard towers hover on the shore of the river, then farther up the bank, and then finally atop the steep cliff overlooking the river. "Its physical appearance is frowning and terrible," a former inmate once wrote. "Its buildings are low-squatting, resembling the lines of a bull dog."

Indeed, Folsom growls at visitors, however long they plan to stay. Inside, sharply textured granite walls are as thick as the length of a man, and they rise to high ceilings that stretch out over the inmates like a steel sky. Windows line the top walls, far out of reach of the prisoners, permitting only a muted light which drifts down to the cell block floors, like a fog. The dirty glow inside reveals a maze, a series of box-like rooms and rifle-barrel corridors through which citizens circulate from cell to job to mess hall to exercise yard to cell. Halfway up the walls, perched on gunwalks, unsmiling prison guards peer down on the daily commute, ready to cut down with their polished rifles anyone who would disrupt the gray routine.

A Folsom guard pacing the catwalk, 1968.
(Photo by Jim Marshall)

(upper left) Folsom Prison

(upper right) Folsom Prison guard John Cologna, c. 1920s

(left) The lower yard and rock quarry of Folsom Prison, early twentieth century.

(Courtesy of the author's collection)

The Lower Yard & Rock Quarry,
Folsom State Prison.
Folsom Calif.

   Although Folsom State Prison is actually located in appropriately named Repressa, California, it takes its name from Folsom, California. When Cash first visited in the 1960s, before strip malls and tony subdivisions with pretentious names took over, Folsom was a husk of a gold mining town, silent and far away from the vitality of Sacramento and San Francisco. Although the town lay barely a mile from its namesake, in Cash's day it might as well have been separated from the prison by the tallest peaks in the nearby Sierra Nevadas. It was, like the prison, a city unto itself.

The discovery of gold along the American River in the late 1840s attracted thousands to the area that would become Folsom, including its original inhabitants (post–Gold Rush, anyway): a group of black forty-niners whose riverside encampment became known as Negro Bar. Joseph Libby Folsom, a wily and persistent former army captain who owned tracts of land along the river and made a fortune loaning money to gold-hungry speculators, first conceived of Folsom under the name Granite City. He envisioned a railroad town growing up on the bluffs above encamped gold diggers. And because he sat on the board of the Sacramento Valley Railroad in San Francisco, his vision wasn't so difficult to realize. He influenced the laying of a route that terminated in Folsom and hired an engineer named Theodore Dehone Judah to map out a town. But the Captain never touched the form of his vision. He died in 1855, leaving his heirs to construct the dream that *they* called Folsom.

Thanks to the railroad rather than the shimmering metals that miners were scratching from the riverbed below, Joseph Folsom's vision proved golden. The Folsom depot became a transportation hub where the eastbound Sacramento line met stage and freight lines headed toward the Nevada mother lode, an even bigger cache of gold which glinted to the east in the heart of the Sierra Nevadas. For a time in the early 1860s, Folsom was the western terminus for the Pony Express. Miners, merchants, and railroad men streamed into Folsom.

The prison joined the burgeoning Folsom community in 1880 after a power company that sought to dam the American River offered the state of California 350 acres of land outside Folsom to build a prison in exchange for convict labor to help build the dam. After protracted political wrangling among state prison officials and legislators over whether or not to build anew in Folsom or expand the Golden State's first prison in San Quentin, the convict labor agreement was sealed and construction on Folsom commenced in 1878. Two years later, Folsom's first cell block completed, the prison welcomed its first inmate, an arsonist named Chong Hing.

Behind Folsom's forbidding medieval edifice, a veritable city sprawled. In an era when convict labor was the accepted form of punishment and rehabilitation, inmates scattered each day to jobs in the prison's ice plant, dairy, farm, or slaughterhouse, while the less fortunate pulverized rocks in the prison's commercial granite quarry. In 1888, a detail of prison inmates were dispatched to build a rush off of the American River in order to power an electrical generation plant, which for the first time in the United States would bring electricity to a prison. Behind the walls of this city, yet out of reach of the inmates, were 350 homes for staff and their families, a gas station, and a store. While one would hardly call Folsom the Paris of incarceration's world, it far exceeded the cramped, rat-infested San Quentin as a model of humane prison conditions.

But Folsom was a maximum security prison. As the mortar between the blocks in the newly built prison hardened, so did its culture. Ed Morrell, the self-proclaimed vigilante bank robber whom Jack London immortalized in his novel *The Star Rover,* landed in Folsom in the first years of the 1900s. Writing about his experiences inside after his pardon, he called Folsom a "Man Killing Jail," a hole where many would rather die than go on living. "Convicts not hardened to endure its slave racking toil and tortures have deliberately faced the guns of their eager executioners, ... have blindly hurled themselves into the rushing waters of the River to go down at least to a more merciful death. Such tragedies were common at the time I entered Folsom." Punishment at Folsom was harsh. A show of disrespect once landed Morrell in the derrick, the punishment chamber, where guards handcuffed him and hung him by the wrists for seven days. Not long after, in an attempt to wheedle a confession from him, they battered him and later burned lime around his cell, a torture that inflamed his eyes, nose, mouth, and internal organs. Morrell saw guards club men at will and, in a particularly appalling moment, shoot two inmates who jumped into the roiling American River to rescue another inmate.

A hard place of hard guards, the prisoners too were hard, and they matched their captors, wit for wit. In Morrell's time, a band of daredevil men shamelessly counterfeited money under the warden's and guards' noses, and still others planned intricate escapes, fashioning weapons from scraps of metal and tapping allies to plant weapons in the nearby hills. Mutiny loomed; the murderers, rapists, and robbers were more than capable of it.

By the 1920s, tales of the danger that permeated Folsom drifted into American society, crowning Folsom over the ensuing decades with a dubious celebrity akin to Al Capone's and Bruno Hauptmann's. Newspapers followed the ugly matron on the hill with perverse fascination, waiting for reports of the latest uprising or bizarre tale to emerge. And the public lapped it up.

The prison proved to have a mystery all of its own, a legendary place in California folklore, indeed in American folklore, in part because of its legendary inmates. At one time or another, Folsom housed the West's most notorious criminals: Ed Davis, who ran with Pretty Boy Floyd, "Little Pete" Fong Ching, the mafia kingpin of San Francisco's Chinatown, and George Sontag, a feared Wells Fargo bank robber.

In 1927, Americans opened their newspapers to read the chronicle of a daring mutiny at Folsom, in which seven died and 22 were injured. Ten years later, history repeated itself. Five inmates attempted to bust out and killed warden Clarence Larkin. They were caught and executed. Reported in still other newspaper stories were an inmate who died after being restricted in a straight jacket, a death row inmate who wrote a mawkish poem to his mother before he was hanged, a murderer of his eight wives who landed in Folsom, an inmate who willed a third of his estate to a San Francisco resident whom he'd never met—if he agreed to attend his funeral. Such stories rolled out frequently in the press, but none proved as bizarre as Ernest Booth's, a bank robber and writer who played chicken with the heavy gates of Folsom Prison. Seemingly a successful reform story, Ernest Booth had been published while behind bars by H. L. Mencken in the *American Mercury* and also had written a ballyhooed novel, *Stealing Through Life*. In 1937, largely because of his writing, he received parole. Booth was like many Folsom inmates who throughout its history wrote to cope with boredom or with an eye on redemption, and soon after he walked freely, he went to work in Hollywood, where he wrote pulpy films such as *Penrod's Double Trouble* and *The Men of San Quentin*. But to the delight of America's scandal mongers, Booth returned to his old ways. In 1941, police arrested the screenwriter on suspicion of bludgeoning to death Florence Stricker, a Los Angeles heiress. He dodged the charge, only to be convicted two years later in connection with a $250,000 securities theft. But the verdict was reversed. It wasn't much later, though, that Booth's foxy luck fizzled out. In 1947, a jury sent him to San Quentin for armed robbery.

The coverage of Folsom was better than a serial mystery.

However, by the 1960s, different stories emerged from Folsom. Although the nation's reporters still filed stories macabre, dramatic, and loony (such as a hostage taking in the prison chapel or the arrest of a would-be escapee who had tried to make a helicopter), the story about Folsom and all prisons across America was reform. As social consciousness awoke from one of its periodic drowsy spells, observers in many stations questioned the effectiveness of incarceration. Lurid stories of earlier decades gave way to serious reporting about prisons, which many had come to realize were merely crime schools or, at best, dead ends. Reports chronicling ugly and potentially explosive conditions regularly slipped through the nation's prison walls: ridiculously long sentences, prison riots, and slave-like working conditions. Investigators in Cash's home state of Arkansas discovered a torture device which "consisted of a crank telephone and a generator wired to an inmate's big toe and scrotum"; this incredible invention used in the 1960s was the brainchild of a prison doctor.

By almost unanimous consent, prisons were condemned. Even the California Department of Corrections' own studies questioned the effectiveness of prison rehabilitation efforts, confirming what any prisoner or prison administrator already knew: that the penitentiaries launched men and women back into a world of crime, only to see them boomerang back again. "I can think of no prison in the United States that really does its job," wrote Bruce Jackson, a professor who researched prison effectiveness in the 1960s. "The best—like Californian and Texas—do what they can, but they are trapped in a conceptual nightmare created by outsiders who neither understand the prison's potential nor care very much about its limitations. As long as prisons are filled with inmates who should not be there and as long as prison administrations are handed the job of patching or hiding the

major failures of other social agencies, they are going to continue failing."
Recidivism rates across the nation stood at 70 percent in 1968, embarrassing
proof of the American prison system's failure.

In California, many legislators and prison administrators were ready to
knock down the prison walls, proposing support of institutions without
walls where convicts could move about freely and enjoy conjugal visits. For
others who studied the prison question, wholesale parole of thousands of
inmates was the answer. "There is evidence," said a legislative report, "that
larger numbers of offenders can be effectively supervised in the community,
at insignificant risk and considerable savings in public expense." The same
report recommended shuttering San Quentin. And where would Quentin's
most violent and depraved go, the ones for whom parole was out of the
question? Folsom. Nobody spoke of closing Folsom.

Sociologists and the like who studied failing prisons in the 1960s need
only to have looked at Folsom for a model. On paper, the prison offered
hope in the form of training programs, education, work skills, and counseling—and many seized those opportunities—but below the cellblocks that
towered five levels high, there was a hole where murder, prostitution, and
hatred—personal and racial—thrived. An inside-inside prison, the max, its
prisoners saw nobody but each other, the guards, and a few staffers, unlike
the boys of lower-security San Quentin or Vacaville who interacted with
more free people, administration employees, and others at prison-wide ban-
quets and employee-inmate baseball games. But above the American River,
there were long-bill hats, frowns, and grunted acknowledgments.
"Everybody had that old, mean look on their faces," said one lifer.

The prisoners in Folsom were old hands in the criminal justice system,
many on their second, third, fourth go-rounds, some aspiring to live out
their lives behind bars despite whatever vague legislated promise of freedom
lay in front of them. "Why should I want to leave?" cracked one Folsom
denizen in 1968. "I run the block. I'm a millionaire in cigarettes. I can get all

the ice cream I want. My sex life is different from yours, but you get used to that." The men of Folsom were older, rarely under 25 or 30. They were killers, rapists, three-time losers, four-time losers, even. They had reached the end of the line, or they were nearing it.

Millard Dedmon lived amid the pallor of Folsom, in a four-and-a-half-foot-wide cell. A Los Angeles native with a bulging file in the offices of the California Youth Authority—he entered reform school in 1953 on a marijuana charge—Dedmon had landed in Folsom after kidnapping a woman in Santa Barbara in 1960. Because the young man had used a shotgun and injured the woman whom he'd kidnapped, he fell under the minimum sentencing requirements of California's little Lindbergh law, which cut little slack for kidnappers who injured their victims; Dedmon received life without parole. Because of Dedmon's sentence and his time in the Department of Corrections' farm system, he was sent to Folsom at the tender age of 25. Another young man might be quickly "turned out" by sex-deprived veterans, but, as Dedmon puts it, "They thought I was sophisticated enough to handle the prison environment."

Inmate Millard Dedmon (with trumpet) stays cool at Folsom in the 1960s.
(Courtesy of Millard Dedmon)

Younger prisoners—less sophisticated than Dedmon, one presumes—generally were diverted away from Folsom because of the fights they'd spark among leering older convicts eager to rape them or claim them for pimping. A retired corrections officer's recollections illustrate the point: "Years ago we had a young inmate in San Quentin. He was pressured by another inmate for homosexual favors, and the guy kept sayin' 'No.' He knocked out the inmate in the head, got tried, got additional time, and was transferred to Folsom to get him away from the other inmate. So he comes to Folsom Prison and he aligns himself, I'm talking about convict type marriages. And the two of them, they became very friendly, and they were noted for being a couple. Another older inmate, he tried to convince the younger inmate that, 'Hey, you should become my friend and partner 'cause I could do more for you, I can treat you better.' And so the two guys that were together, they kept telling this guy, 'Leave us alone. Leave us alone.' So they killed him. They were tried, convicted, sentenced to death."

If lascivious men eyed Dedmon, there were also gangs who could either protect him from them or act as his pimp. All in all, though, Dedmon avoided denimed suitors without the help of gangs, but from behind his black-rimmed glasses he saw quickly that gangs wielded mighty control over the inside world.

Like the gangs he knew in the outside world, Folsom's packs were divided along racial lines, their names giving away their ethnic affiliation: the Black Guerilla Family, the Aryan Brotherhood, the Mexican Mafia, the San Antonio Family. Sustained by racism and fear, the gangs protected the weaker of their ethnicity and controlled a vibrant trade in prostitution, drug dealing, gambling, and extortion—all within the prison walls, thanks to corrupt prison guards and good contacts on the outside and in the mail room who could traffic drugs and money in and out of the granite city. Many sought out gangs because they only knew the gang life, while others hid behind their protection or took refuge in the pseudo-family that they were. A member of the Aryan Brotherhood at Folsom says his fraternity mentored its own: "We built all the white boys that were weak.... It stopped them from being turned into queers. It stopped them from gettin' their property stolen. If they were bringing drugs in, you know, it stopped them from being ripped off of 'em." Of course, the gangs skimmed a percentage whenever the protection protected money. Otherwise, protection bought loyalty.

Gangs brought a strange sense of order to Folsom. In the absence of city blocks, train tracks, and other demarcations of turf, skin color chalked lines through the prison. And although the lines sometimes became battle lines, they sometimes preserved the peace. Gang justice cooled hot heads and subdued brewing violence throughout Folsom. Leaders worked with each other like diplomats of clashing super powers to avoid bloody riots, but their cold war solutions could prove bizarre and tragic. A former Folsom guard recalls an incident when to settle up with the Aryan Brotherhood, the Black Guerilla Family preyed on its own man: "There was one incident, an old black man that lived in Two Building.... They killed him just so that the debt would be even in the eyes of the rest of the inmate population. 'We took care of the problem so there's no riot, there's no war.' They sacrificed some little old black man just so there wouldn't be any more problem between the two gangs.... But that satisfied the Aryan Brotherhood. 'That was okay, we saved face 'cause we went and told you to take care of it and you did.' Everything revolves around respect and disrespect when it comes to gangs."

In the spirit of uneasy cooperation, gangs also united against common enemies: they refused to testify against one another in criminal proceedings stemming from their squabbles, and they attacked child molesters like blood-thirsty soccer thugs lunging at an erring referee. If there was a code among all prisoners at Folsom—among prisoners everywhere in America—it was death to child molesters. As if on cue, gangs led charges on them, marauding among the marked ones, slashing, beating, killing, anything to yank them off the main line. They'd spot those who bragged of their per-verse crimes, or trustees would rifle though files to identify them, or they'd learn who was who from the guards—and then the blood flowed. "We took care of, like, 250 within two weeks, and it hardly ever got in the newspaper," brags a former Folsom gang shark. "Nobody ever went to court over it.

Bunch of us got locked up at one time for a few weeks.... They just let it stand. They let it go by, and just as well. Those guys ain't no good anyway. You know, they're rats." Once the warden determined a molester stood to have his heart carved out, he'd be transferred out of the prison or locked away in the security housing unit, the jail inside the prison. Beating molesters—like settling a gang score—earned gang and prison-wide respect.

Despite the gangs' omnipresence, Folsom was known as a place where one could do his own time, remain unaffiliated. Like Millard Dedmon. The Black Guerilla Family courted him, but a brief stint mediating between the Aryan Brotherhood and the Guerillas was the closest he ever came to gang involvement. Dedmon's brand of trouble at Folsom was not of the gang stripe: he once landed in isolation for loaning his typewriter to a friend.

Dedmon, a tall, muscular dude, scythed his own path through the caged world, haunting the prison library to work up an appeal of his conviction, reading books on black history and politics, cutting meat in the butcher shop, and rapping with Black Panther Eldridge Clever, an old friend from his California Youth Authority days, who in the 1960s was writing *Soul on Ice* while an inmate at Folsom. In Folsom, Dedmon found detention so much more excruciating than his youth incarceration. And he struggled to cope with it, dreaming of liberty, of a woman or the corner store where he'd pick up an ice cream or a beer. He was apoplectic in the midst of the vacant inmates he saw muttering to themselves, and to the wall, and to the sky, men driven from reality by imprisonment.

For as long as he could, he veered away from the interpersonal conflict that—along with gangs and insanity—came with prison life. All around him there were blow-ups over gambling debts, stolen cigarettes, and angry words. Violence often stilled the prison yard, as shanks plunged into stomachs, and bodies lay on the ground. Those glinting knives frequently broke the darkness of movie times in the dining hall when deathly cries stopped the projectors and inmates stepped around pools of blood. Dedmon's fellow inmate Earl Green saw a man stabbed to death as punishment for kicking a cat. "The guy [who took care of the cat] seen him," says Green. "Next day the guy killed him."

Over time, Dedmon learned to keep his mind where his body was, dismissing the call of freedom. "When I first got there, the first few years, maybe two-three years, I was often thinking about the outside and dreaming and wishing and all that kind of thing. But you learn to get away from that kind of thing because that's not the thing that's gonna be able to help you stay there and cope with your situation. You got to be a realist." Dedmon's mind closed around the stone-and-steel coffer that stored his body, playing jazz trumpet in the band room and chapel, studying for a high school diploma, or chilling out listening to the prison radio station through an ear piece that plugged into his cell wall.

All prisoners coped in their own way, with gangs, with dealing in drugs and prostitution, by gambling. Men forgot the absence of women with their sissy or by huddling in their cell with their porn. "You missed cuddling with a woman," says a former inmate. "You miss your family. Yeah, they come and visit but it's not like kicking back on the couch with your arm around your mom and dad."

There were those who sought chemical escape, through the drugs that were smuggled in or through the champagne of prison life, a putrid concoction known as pruno. Imbibers of pruno nicked the ingredients from the kitchen—oranges, ketchup, sugar, and copped yeast from the bakery—and mixed it all in a six-gallon milk bag used in cafeteria milk dispensers. Duct taping a hose from the bag and running it into the toilet to hide the fumes, the slimy mixture would be covered by a blanket and stored under the bunk. Concerned that the hacks would smell and discover the fermenting ingredients, prisoners unceasingly scrubbed their cells with Comet or something with a bleachy smell. Prison moonshiners could cook up a six-gallon bag in about three days and trade it for cigarettes, sex, money. It delivered a stupefying bender.

What perhaps was more stupefying than the pruno was that all such manner of lawbreaking thrived in a prison, where men were supposed to be reformed of the criminal life. Under the always scanning eyes of prison guards, it seemed unlikely that a prisoner could run his fingertips up and down the bars of his cell without going unnoticed. The guards appeared omnipresent, absent only in education classes and the hospital. Prisoners weren't necessarily escorted everywhere—like when they walked between their prison building and the yard, or to the dining room—but eyes peered down from the gunwalks that surrounded almost every prison space. "In your cell, you look up and a man on the gun rail is passing by, maybe standing looking into your cell," remembers Dedmon. "So you're under the gun everywhere. In the dining room, mess hall, you're under the gun. In the yard, anywhere you go, you're under the gun." Their eyes and their Winchester 30-30s were like x-rays, stripping the prisoners of their privacy, reducing them to fish in a bowl. Plenty of times those rifles cracked with fire, to disperse big fights mostly. Warning shots fired in the air echoed sharply through the yard to scatter the rioters, followed by a whistle. If the whistle failed to move the prisoners, the guards fired into the crowd. Prisoners froze when they heard the whistle, or they hit the ground. The sound haunted Millard Dedmon for many years after his release; sporting events or traffic cops were unbearable.

Days for those who meandered through the yards and corridors of Folsom ended early. Everybody was ordered back to their cells for lockdown and count at 3:20. Twice in the evening they were released, for dinner and showers. Bodies were counted once more, before lights dimmed at ten o'clock. Then restless silence unfolded over the cell blocks, interrupted by hacking coughs, the jangle of guards, and muted conversations. Folsom slept, until sunrise and the next morning's count.

"Folsom was a graveyard to me," says Millard Dedmon. "There was nothing about Folsom that I liked."

Them poor babies were listening to John so hard you could feel it.
    —June Carter Cash on Johnny Cash's 1968 Folsom Prison Concert

0003

In the midst of Cash's hiatus from recording and search for sobriety in the late months of 1967, Columbia Records ushered out of the Nashville studios their popular country star's producers: Don Law into retirement and Frank Jones into executive management. Law and Jones' big boss, CBS Records president Clive Davis, announced in October that Dylan-producer Bob Johnston would take the A&R reigns of Columbia-Nashville and, accordingly, assume the production of Cash's records. A 36-year-old Texan, Johnston was as crazy as Cash was erratic. He dared to buck authority—one Dylan biographer called him an "irascible opponent of studio executives" —and he ran his recording sessions like a hopped-up carnival barker. Session players stared mystified as the producer jumped on the recording console or rambled on over the studio talk-back. "He was one of those wild, unorganized, near Bohemian, types," observes Don Reid. "I don't know how he ever got it all put together as a record producer. The only thing I remember about him is, no matter what song he was doing, he'd flip the switch on and tell the drummer to lay a wallet on the drum. He wanted to mute that drum so he'd always say, 'Lay a wallet on it.' And the drummer would pull his billfold out and lay it on the drum and he'd say, 'Okay, that's it.'"

From his former base in New York, Johnston had worked up an amazing resume by producing Dylan, Simon and Garfunkel, Leonard Cohen, and others in Columbia's stable of triple crown winners. But he was no stranger to Nashville, having accompanied Dylan to the town for the minstrel's *Blonde on Blonde* and *John Wesley Harding* sessions, sojourns that some surely assumed were a result of Dylan's friendship with Cash. Such speculation, though, is utterly refuted by Johnston: "No ... I was standing in the studio on *Highway 61* and I said, 'Hey man.... You ought to go down to Nashville

Waiting for the cue. Bob Johnston with Cash. (Photo by Jim Marshall)

sometime.' I said, 'They got no clocks and those fucking musicians are great. You'd really enjoy it.' And he said, 'Hmm.' He never answered. He said, 'Oohhh,' like Jack Benny. So when he left the studio, when he walked out, [Bill] Gallagher, [a vice president of CBS] and [Albert] Grossman, his manager, came over and said, 'If you ever say anything to Dylan about Nashville again, you're fired and we'll get somebody else.' I said, 'Why?' He said, 'Because you're successful here. We don't want him down there.' I said, 'Whatever you say. You're the boss.' So [six] months later, I took him down to Nashville and did *Blonde on Blonde*."

From Cash's perspective, this Texas speculator with New York bite appeared to be the gatekeeper who could admit him to a recording date in prison, and he planned to bring up the matter in their first meeting. Throughout the '60s, Cash had raised the idea with Don Law, but Law couldn't or wouldn't sell the idea. It's not that Law frowned upon Cash's recording live—he had prepared to record him at the disastrous Carnegie Hall show in 1962—but it's possible that the aging A&R man failed to see the appeal of a prison show. Or he simply struck out trying to sell the idea to Columbia's brass. One staffer of that era says Cash appealed directly to Columbia Records boss Goddard Leiberson, recalling a terse exchange of letters between frustrated singer and unmoved executive. Columbia's masters, it's likely, feared that any prison connection would taint the label's good name, or, likely too, were skeptical of such an enterprise's sea legs. Whatever the barriers were, Johnston immediately vanquished them. "After six years of talking I finally found the man who would listen at Columbia Records," so wrote Cash in the liner notes to *At Folsom Prison*. "Bob Johnston believed me when I told him that a prison would be *the* place to record an album live." According to Johnston's telling of Cash's plea, the

Reverend Floyd Gressett.
(Photo by Jim Marshall)

singer came to him in his new Nashville office as a mafia don with entourage: "I was sitting in the office one day and a black guy walked in, the janitor, with Cash, through the back door. June and everybody was waiting outside. They were afraid that he was dead or got in a wreck or something because he was, at that point, real high.... He sat down and he says, 'I'm Johnny Cash.' I said, 'How you doin' Johnny?' And he said, 'I wanted to talk to you a minute.' I said, 'Sure.' And he leaned back in his chair and he said, 'I've always wanted to go to prison to record and nobody would let me in eight years and I don't guess you will either.' So ... I picked up the phone and I called Folsom and Quentin, and I got through to Folsom first."

As apocryphal as the above may seem, there is no question that Johnston flashed the green light to the Folsom gambit. And when he did, Cash shifted into gear.

He asked his pastor, Floyd Gressett—who knew well "Coach" Lloyd Kelley, the prison's recreation director—to arrange a date. "I guess I wanted to record in a prison ever since I played Huntsville," Cash told Christopher Wren. "I thought people would take notice of men that have been forgotten in everybody's mind. It would be good for them to hear the men's reaction."

The Man in Black neglected to mention to Wren his calculated guess that a recorded prison encounter would make for damn good theater. Altruism aside, Cash knew he had in prisoners an adoring audience that roared for him and stood with him because he did the same for them and because they knew he'd spent a few nights in the clink (or maybe worse). An element of danger in prison also promised to dramatize his album, a line between safety and hell, which Cash—like a Jumpin' Jack Flash—loved to dance upon. And if the prisoners took him hostage or dared to rise up in some other way? Well, all the more drama then. "That would have thrilled him," says Don Reid, who with the Statlers opened Cash's Folsom show. "If they held him for about five days. He wouldn't have had anything to eat. He would have loved that." Reid further ventures that Cash would have shunned too much security against such flare-ups, or, more to the point, too great a *show* of security. He was there to be one with the prisoners—it was part of the act and reflected his feelings for the men: Any hint of alliance with the guards would have drawn an unerasable line between him and the captured. And, adds Reid, "it wouldn't play to his image to be too heavily guarded."

After 13 years of recording, Cash knew that latent magic could come to life when tape was rolling, in prison or in the studio. Diving into the unknown and waiting for the ripples paid off many times. That's why he ignored convention in the studio, shrugging off producers' advice, forgetting the sacred clock to which recording executives bowed. Don Reid often observed the serendipity that Cash counted on form like a royal flush: "We have seen him go into the studio and actually write songs during the session. He would go totally unprepared and get inspired and write songs. [Then he'd] go get somethin' to eat, and you'd be there all night. He would come up with something, but he didn't necessarily go in with anything." Folsom held the same promise: the gambler's reward. Now, it all might amount to wasted tape, but something absolutely riveting could emerge too. Cash banked on the latter—but took out an insurance policy just in case. His protection against wasted tape laid in the two shows Cash had scheduled at Folsom: 9:40 and 12:40. If the first show failed to move through the morning like the slipstream and leave him with a generally unblemished concert for the album, the magicians in Columbia's studios could create the appearance of such a concert by cutting and pasting the two shows into one.

Bob Johnston may have required a fire policy too. He claimed that his job hung on the line over Folsom: "I remember I got a call from Clive Davis and he said, 'We hear you're taking Cash to prison. If you do, it'll ruin his career and you'll never do business with CBS again.' ... And I said, 'Well, you're the boss.'"

Clearing the way for Columbia Records to bring recording equipment to Folsom meant wading through reams of red tape, but nobody doubted that Cash's request would be welcomed by the prison authorities. After all, his "Folsom Prison Blues" of 1955 had contributed to the prison's infamy, and when he played there for the first time in 1966, the prisoners and corrections officers lapped him up. And how often did a performer of Cash's caliber and celebrity stop by? Rarely. San Quentin, a medium-max security prison, got the bigger names while entertainment at Folsom mostly meant Saturday afternoon movies, a country and western band led by the local sheriff, or the services of visiting evangelists. Cash's performances were welcome anytime, with or without recording equipment. They were, as former corrections officer Jim Brown put it, "a way to forget about what's going on inside. And [you seem to be] outside because somebody from outside is entertaining; they're here. So it's kind of like a chance to escape and forget about where you're at."

Cash's first visit to Folsom in 1966 had ladled up just that kind of escape. Earl Green, the Folsom inmate who'd seen the stabbing over a cat, received counseling from Floyd Gressett and had heard from Gressett early in '66 that Cash wished to perform at Folsom. Green passed the news to

Coach Kelley, who called Gressett to confirm the message that Green had delivered. A Cash visit was a tempting proposition to Kelley's entertainment-bereft community, but he was leery. Didn't Cash carry some baggage? "At the time I was under the impression he was an ex-inmate," he says. After investigating the singer's past and assuring Folsom's authorities that Cash was unlikely to slash the warden or marshal a prison break, Kelley set it up. He performed outside in the prison yard, with Green handling the sound and old Sara Carter of the original Carter Family—who lived nearby in Calaveras County—sitting in with the heirs to her tradition: Mother Maybelle Carter, June Carter, Helen Carter, and Anita Carter.

When Cash brought his show back a year or so later, he'd be walking into a recording session, one in the most unusual of studios. The date was set for Saturday, January 13, 1968.

During the Christmas holidays preceding the Folsom recording date, Cash's latest single "Rosanna's Going Wild" debuted on *Billboard's* country music charts. A jaunty tear through the teenage rebellion of a young girl, presumably his daughter Rosanne, the song was nowhere near his best work: He sounded drawn, sapped perhaps by his drug battles and a vigorous fall touring slate. There was little reason to believe that the record's debut portended a climb to number one because Cash had not reached the top of the charts since mid-1964, when his macho "Understand Your Man" hammered a stake in the spot for six consecutive weeks. The singer's fallow period seems improbable today, when many just assume that Cash dominated country music between the ages of Hank Williams and Garth Brooks. But Cash had skidded into a long, flat dry spell. The four singles prior to "Rosanna" had flickered briefly on the country charts, and no Johnny Cash album containing new material had hit number one since 1964. The likes of Eddy Arnold, Buck Owens, and Charley Pride elbowed Cash out of the way on the country side, leaving him restless perhaps for another "Understand Your Man."

Still, Cash must have been giddy when he and his contingent from Nashville landed in Sacramento for the Folsom rehearsals: the show he had plotted out over many years was only two days away; he was making some progress in his drug war; and his divorce from Vivian Liberto had become final a few days before (after 13 years of marriage that had been undeniably hard on Vivian). He'd gained the freedom to marry June Carter and, thanks to Bob Johnston, had gained the freedom to record in prison. There was good news on the sales front, too: "Rosanna's Going Wild" was surging unexpectedly to the number two mark on the country charts and was making a brief appearance on the pop charts too.

In Sacramento, Cash, June Carter, the Tennessee Three, and the Statler Brothers moved into the El Rancho Inn for two days of rehearsing in one of the hotel's banquet halls. The gang almost never spent so much time preparing for shows, according to Marshall Grant: "We very seldom ever rehearsed while we were on the road at all. And John was famous and notorious for just throwing songs in. All the time he did it. But that's just part of John. But it didn't bother the band because we were always ready for him." However, on January 13TH they would only have one chance—well two, actually—to get it right and, to further complicate matters, Cash was stacking the set list with songs of prison and confinement (including two which he rarely if ever performed), so a little prep work was in order. Dressed casually in sweaters and slacks, amid tables of sandwiches and drinks, the Johnny Cash corps ran through the standards—"Busted," "I Still Miss Someone," "Give My Love to Rose"—and the prison favorites—"Folsom Prison Blues," "Cocaine Blues," "I Got Stripes." But one song sucked up the most practice time: "Greystone Chapel" by an amateur songwriter named Glen Sherley who happened to live at Folsom.

(top) June Carter at the Folsom rehearsals.

(bottom) Glen Sherley.

(Photos by Jim Marshall)

An inmate most of his adult life, Sherley was working at the time in Coach Kelley's issue room, where he checked sports equipment to prisoners. Incarcerated on an armed robbery conviction, Sherley used to strum his guitar for Kelley and, according to Kelley, had been sketching out "Greystone Chapel" in the equipment cage. In the prison chapel, Sherley taped the song and asked Kelly to get it to Floyd Gressett. While prison guards looked the other way—whether intentionally or not, it's unknown—Gressett carried the tape out for delivery to Johnny Cash. Just when Gressett gave the tape to Cash is the subject of some debate. Accounts have it in Cash's hands a year before the show, and others, the night before. In Christopher Wren's telling of these events, Sherley had given Gressett the tape in 1967, but the preacher had waited until the eve of the concert or thereabouts to pass it to Cash.

Whatever the case, Gressett, as he had promised, delivered the tape to Cash, and in rehearsals, Cash, the Statlers, June, and the band worked up an arrangement opened by Carl Perkins' country-funky opening licks. An anthem for the imprisoned, "Greystone Chapel" describes the mind that with Christ has transcended its cell. *Inside the walls of prison, my body may be/But the Lord has set my soul free*. It promised to be the perfect climax in the drama Cash planned to stage, a message of redemption dispatched by the very criminal mind he'd be entertaining.

In the Folsom community, inmate Sherley cut a gaunt figure, not unlike Cash's. Born to Oklahoma farm workers in 1936, Milburn Glen Sherley migrated with his family to California in the 1940s, where they picked cotton, potatoes, and any other crop within their reach. But the promised land was tired dirt for young Glen. By the early 1950s, his was a regular face in the state's juvenile justice system, and when he joined the army seeking some direction in life, little changed: He spent most of his stint in the brig. Throughout the late 1950s and 1960s, he swung around in prison's revolving door, robbing banks and liquor stores—often with a toy gun—and earning in return a tour of the Golden State's prisons. He marked time in Soledad, and San Quentin, and by 1967 had finally made the big leagues, earning a bed in Folsom after too many small-time jobs and a daring jailbreak. "He and another fellow had been picked up for robbery of some kind and were put in jail ... ," explains Sherley's stepson Rusty Courtney. "They found an opportunity to break jail ... and, as I understand it, he made it all the way to Oklahoma where he was ratted out by either a friend or a family member. ... It got a little bit more serious, and [they] sent him to maximum security." A brooding inmate with violent tendencies, Sherley wasn't all that different from his fellow denizens, at least until Johnny Cash tried "Greystone Chapel" on for size. "He was a typical inmate," remembers Coach Kelley. " ... He never created any trouble. The fact is I don't remember ever having any infraction against him."

On the outside, during brief respites from crime and prison, Sherley had shown some interest in the guitar and songwriting, picking them up with gusto, out of boredom perhaps, when he got to Folsom. "It was a way to pass time," reckons another stepson, Keith Sherley. "I don't really think that he ever saw it as anything, as a way to make a living." An artistic beehive where many inmates painted, sculpted, or wrote poetry, Folsom's cavernous halls also rang with music. Prisoners blew trumpets, beat drums, sang in choirs, creating jazz, gospel, and, of course, country and western. Sherley joined Folsom's fraternity of musicians, strumming in his cell and recording jam sessions on the prison chapel's tape machine. If music was helping Sherley pass time, it was also flying him over the ominous walls around him, if only mentally. Music could effect escape for prisoners, as Sherley knew—and for free men, as Cash knew.

The Folsom rehearsals.

(top) Left to right, surrounding Cash: Johnston, Grant (partially obscured), unknown, June Carter, Don Reid, Harold Reid, Philip Balsley, Lew Dewitt.

(bottom) Left to right, surrounding Bob Johnston: Cash, Grant (partially obscured), Carl Perkins, W. S. Holland, Floyd Gressett.

(Photos by Jim Marshall)

As Cash's troupe plowed through the last rehearsal in Sacramento, a tuxedoed gent with jet black hair and a hardy gait popped his head in the door to greet Cash. The boss of the Department of Corrections and everything else in California state government, Gov. Ronald Reagan ushered in an air of glitter in what were otherwise gritty practice sessions. Celebrity biographer Albert Govoni wrote about the scene:

> At that moment, Johnny Cash, singing into a mike about thirty feet away, looked up and spotted the state's chief executive. Johnny waved, whipped his guitar behind his back in that familiar downsweep motion, and walked over to the door. He had met Reagan before, but he greeted him the way he does everyone.
>
> Extending his big right paw to shake the governor's hand, he said affably, "Hello Governor—I'm Johnny Cash."
>
> Reagan shook the hand warmly and grinning from ear to ear, quipped, "You're telling me."
>
> They exchanged a few words, then Reagan asked interestedly, with a nod toward the performers singing and playing all over the big banquet room, "How's it going?"
>
> Johnny glanced around, then said easily, "We'll make it. We're kinda busy right now, but you know how it is—it'll all come together at once."

(clockwise from below left) June Carter at the Folsom rehearsals.

The Folsom rehearsals. Left to right, surrounding Cash: Holland (in foreground), unknown, Gressett (partially obscured), Johnston, Carter, Don Reid, Harold Reid (partially obscured), Balsley, Dewitt.

The Folsom rehearsals. Left to right: Cash, Harold Reid, Ray Cash, Don Reid, Balsley.

(Photos by Jim Marshall)

After Reagan swept out of the room, Cash ran through a few more songs and retired for five hours of sleep. The next morning, Cash revisited Sherley's song, and by seven o'clock he, June, Bob Johnston, and Cash's father Ray were in limousines traveling 25 miles northeast to Folsom. The others rode in the large camper that Cash usually took on the road. Hours before, two veteran Columbia engineers based in Hollywood—Bill Britain and Bob Breault—had arrived to set up the boxes of recording equipment, running cable between a small makeshift recording room and the dining hall where a wooden stage draped with a welcome banner and straddled by two shotgun-toting guards

awaited the performers and audience. Under a blanket of gray clouds, while the engineers toiled inside, the convoy wended up the driveway to the forlorn Folsom Prison city. Coach Kelley and a sparse crowd of photographers and off-duty guards waited to greet them. One of the guards had crossed paths with Cash years before at San Quentin where the singer performed with a nagging cold. Ten years later, he stopped Cash in front of the gates. Was he feeling better this day? Cash nodded.

(top) The Folsom rehearsals. Left to right, around Cash: Johnston, Carter, Don Reid, Harold Reid (partially obscured), Philip Balsley (partially obscured), Lew Dewitt, Marshall Grant.

(bottom) Ray Cash.

(Photos by Jim Marshall)

Amid the small group of people documenting Cash's arrival were photographer Jim Marshall, whom Columbia hired to shoot photos for the planned album, and *Los Angeles Times* reporter Robert Hilburn, who would write liner notes for the first single from the concert and pen a feature story on the concert for his paper. The news media in San Francisco, Sacramento, and Folsom virtually ignored the buzz at Folsom as did the Department of Corrections' own newsletters and press releases. Only an Up with People extravaganza at lucky ol' medium-max San Quentin got attention in the official prison press.

Free from the media's intense gaze, Cash posed uneasily for a few photographs at the main gate before boarding a prison bus that drove them deep into the sprawling compound. Five guards hovered around them. Everybody appeared worried. Stepping off the bus a few moments later, the lines in Cash's face deepened and shadows of the grim buildings darkened further his black figure. As he looked around outside the bus, his face expressed either trepidation or determination. The Statler Brothers tried with jokes and teasing to gas up the mood, but found few takers: The entire troupe made their way in with few smiles. Cash's eyes drooped into his cheeks, while June—normally so effervescent—cast her head and eyes toward the asphalt ground. When one of many gates crashed behind them, Cash addressed Jim Marshall: "Jim, there's a feeling of permanence to that sound." Marshall—who'd shot a man in Frisco some years before but ducked a heavy sentence—agreed.

(opposite clockwise from top) Outside the prison bus that will take Cash inside.

Walking to the gate. Left to right: Dewitt, Don Reid, Cash, Carter, Ray Cash.

Dewitt clowns. Johnston and m.c. Hugh Cherry chat. Carl Perkins (partially obscured) is at the far left.

(below) Cash arriving at Folsom amid photographers and unidentified corrections officials.

(Photos by Jim Marshall)

(upper left) Cherry leading the somber troupe deeper into Folsom.

(upper right) Left to right: Lloyd "Coach" Kelly, unidentified photographer, Cash, Robert Hilburn of the *Los Angeles Times*, Floyd Gressett, two unidentified.

(Photos by Jim Marshall)

(bottom left)
Funeral procession.

(below)
Walking the line. Carl Perkins follows behind Cash.

(Photos by Jim Marshall)

The Johnny Cash entourage rumbled out of Folsom with ore from which record industry gold would soon be extracted, but what the group carried *in* the gates that morning could have torpedoed the recording before it began.

When Bob Johnston learned he'd be searched upon entering the prison, he thought "drug charges." Rifling through his boots and pockets checking for stray joints, he caught Cash's eye. "Cash said, 'What are you doin'?' I said, 'I'm just looking through my pockets.' And he laughed, and we went on up." One assumes Cash's pockets were empty, too.

Marshall Grant could feel smug about the others' drugs worries, but when he opened his bass guitar case inside the prison, any smugness instantly vanished. He gasped. A pistol glared back at him from inside the case. "John and I always did a little comedy routine together, and in this routine we had a thing where John would do an impersonation of Elvis and then he had to borrow my comb to fix his hair back, and then I would look at the comb like there was a booger on it. And I'd throw it at the floor and pull this big ol' cap and ball gun out that would make a lot of smoke, but it was a real gun. And I would shoot this comb, and it went over real well." On the road Grant tended to Cash's details, but his thoroughness lapsed on this count. "I just didn't think about it.... I opened the thing up and there lay that big 'ol gun, and here I am inside a prison. And I started shakin' in my boots 'cause I didn't know what was getting ready to happen to me here. So one of the guards was standin' there and I closed the case back, ... and I said [to the guard], 'Now it's in that case right there. The inmates just brought it in. I wasn't thinking.' And I'm sittin' here with a real gun inside the walls of Folsom Prison. And he said, 'Let me see it.' And I didn't know if they were gonna arrest me, hang me, or what. But he was very nice about it. He said, 'Well, Mr. Grant, what we can do is take the gun. I'll take it to the warden, and he will keep it in safe-keeping until you finish and then I will bring it outside the gate and hand it back to you.'

"That was a big relief to me, but that's just exactly what happened. But when anybody asks me [if] I remember anything that happened at Folsom Prison that's the first thing I always tell them 'cause it sort of sticks out like a sore thumb."

They had been told by guards that Folsom didn't negotiate with hostage takers, so they knew that conspiracies to grab them could end bloodily. Such warnings set a mind to thinking, as did concerns for June's safety and uncertainty about just how this show would go. Dressed in black and striding somberly, they appeared to be a funeral procession making its way from church to graveyard: Cash the priest, Carter the mourning widow, the rest—Cash's father Ray, the Statler Brothers, the band—pall bearers. "It was an eerie thing," says Marshall Grant.

Inside, the prison guards escorted the Cash entourage to a makeshift dressing room off of the kitchen where the funereal disappeared. Smiles returned. It felt safe. Cash strummed his guitar and sipped coffee; Marshall clowned with June's winter hat; Johnston hammed it up for the photogs; and an old man or two took turns flirting with June, who was now sparkling in her Appalachian beauty. However, not all decompressed. Luther sat to the side on a bench, nibbling a sandwich, as stoic then as he always was on stage, and Carl Perkins, who detested giving his time to lawbreakers, squirmed nearby.

Outside the dressing-room cocoon where Cash and his gypsy circus mingled, in the real Folsom, morning had broken differently.

At 7:00—mandatory waking time—a dull light drifted into the cell blocks of Folsom. Millard Dedmon—who often read in the dimness—and a few other prisoners had risen long before daybreak, but most stirred grudgingly, crawling from their beds to stand at their cell doors and wait to be counted. "Count time," a voice thundered over the public address system, an alarm for those still in their nest. After a northern California winter's

(clockwise from below left)
"What's that you said?" Cash with Don Reid and the bare back of another Statler Brother.

Backstage, Cash's nick heals as Johnston spiels.

Tuning up. Left to right: Cash, Holland, Balsley, Grant.

(Photos by Jim Marshall)

(clockwise from top right) Luther Perkins, nonplussed as ever.

Carl Perkins marks time; Cherry and Johnston with Hilburn.

June waits backstage.

(opposite) Comparing legs, waiting for the cue: Left to right: Harold Reid, Carter, Balsley, Don Reid, Dewitt.

(Photos by Jim Marshall)

night, which had slipped in through busted windows and ancient doorways, cold concrete floors and steel doors extended a cruel greeting. Standing to meet their counter, the men tightly pulled blankets around their shoulders and kicked away the cardboard that they had leaned bed-level against the cell door to block the night's draft.

When the clicking heels of the counting guards had passed, the inmates awaited the rustling of one of their own, the trustee—also known as the tiertender or keyman—who carried hot water. Trolling the corridors, he stopped at each cell and siphoned the water from a large bucket into a gallon bucket that the inmates held inside their cells. It was the one humanizing touch of the morning, steaming water for their bird bath. At 7:30, the inmates left their cells for breakfast before dispersing to their jobs, to their recreation in the yard, or back to their cells. The group of 1,000 prisoners

slated to attend the 9:40 show made their way to dining room #2. Few inmates chose to miss Johnny Cash that day. "Everybody was there," recalls Millard Dedmon. " ... This is escape from the inside. You're getting into a situation that's more like the kind of recreational thing or the entertainment thing that you would be able to choose, to enjoy, on the streets, in the free world. Whenever the opportunity presented itself, I mean everybody just flocked to the shows and things."

For this show, all of Folsom was in preparation. Sherley—who'd been cleared to attend both shows—braced himself for his meeting with Cash; the associate warden gathered a few mementoes to present to the singer after the show; and the Columbia engineers checked and rechecked microphone levels as they made ready to tape on their four-track machines.

The morning was accentuated by the promise of Cash and his concert, but throughout the cold-steel facility, as always, eyes remained open for trouble. Only two weeks before two inmates had punched a guard, gagged him, and held him at knifepoint in an effort to get at an inmate whom they accused of snitching. Tensions were high in the wake, and evidently remained so, even with Cash's intervening concert: A few weeks after Cash left, an inmate work stoppage spread through the prison, drawing the aim of the guard's wary eyes and their polished Winchesters.

(below left) Marshall Grant clowning with June Carter's hat, Folsom Prison, January 13, 1968.

(below right) "Never seen one like this before." Cash with Perkins and Kelley.

(Photos by Jim Marshall)

(clockwise from below left)
Noshing.

Sittin' 'round the dishwasher.

"One for the money, two for the show..." Carl Perkins makes for the stage.

(Photos by Jim Marshall)

As 9:40 approached, guards watched for knives, for fights. There was no reason to believe that at the Cash show a score wouldn't be settled or some nut wouldn't lunge at June or Johnny. But the hall filled without incident. Dismissed from the cellblocks tier by tier, black, white, Hispanic filed in, jostling for a good view. Bob Johnston surveyed them all, futilely trying to make eye contact:

> I stood by the door and watched all the convicts come in and go out. I looked at them, and out of all of those people who came and went, there was not one convict who looked you in the eye. And I asked one of the guys there, I said, "Why is that?" He said, "Because if you look somebody in the eye they're going to say 'Do I know you?' or 'What the fuck are you on?' And then it starts and somebody gets a shove." So he said that's the way that that works there, and that's the reason why. So I went up to some guy, I think his name was Chester, little bitty guy, bad teeth, hundred and forty, eye glasses, and I said, "What are you in here for?" And there was three guards standing there, and he said, "I beat three men to death with a baseball bat. By God, I'd do it again if I had the chance. Fucking people." And the guard said, "Calm down, calm down." And I said, "Wow." And he didn't even look like he could win a fight, much less beat three people to death with a baseball bat.

If the second show was Johnston and Cash's primary insurance policy against a lackluster concert, M.C. Hugh Cherry was his secondary policy. A great supporter of Cash from the 1950s when he was among the first disc jockeys on the West Coast to spin the Sun sensation's records, Cherry took charge of guaranteeing that the prisoners knew they were to cheer and howl and roar throughout the show. "Respond," he pleaded with the prisoners minutes before Carl Perkins took the stage. "You are a part of the album. You are a very important part, and if you hear something you like react in kind." In the absence of the kind of ruffian reaction Cherry was attempting to scare up, Johnston, Cash, and everybody knew the live prison album would be altogether flaccid.

Cherry gave way to Carl Perkins, who shot off a rousing version of "Blue Suede Shoes" to explosive applause. "Let's see how loud 1,000 men

(top) Hugh Cherry brings on Carl Perkins.

(bottom) "You can do anything but lay off of my blue suede shoes."

(following pages)
Glen Sherley, second from the left in the front row, watches the rockabilly legend.

(Photos by Jim Marshall)

(opposite) The Statler Brothers.

(left) "I shot a man in Reno."

(Photos by Jim Marshall)

Cash is next.

(Photos by Jim Marshall)

BLOW MY BLUES AWAY

(top) "Ain't it somethin', Bob." Johnston and Hilburn watch from stage left.

(Photos by Jim Marshall)

from Folsom can be," barked Cherry in the rockabilly hero's wake. "Let's hear it." The decibels shot to the roof. Only Cash seemed not to respond. From the side of the stage against the white-washed granite walls, he stretched and shuffled about as he watched the action unfold. "As relaxed as a bug in a Roach Motel," he said later about the day, Cash wondered if he could pull off the show without his usual handful of pills, although Marshall Grant figures that the star was only about 75 percent straight that day. Bob Johnston stood next to Cash, clenching a slender cigar in his mouth, while the Statlers sauntered to the mic to follow Carl Perkins.

As the quartet crooned, the engineers frantically worked to balance the microphone levels while cranking up the amplification so people in the back could hear everything (and therefore react raucously to everything). But the right sound proved elusive. The show halted, and the Statlers stepped back from their spots. The prisoners groaned, bringing Harold Reid back to his mic. "This is part of your punishment," he joked, "so everybody stay real still." After a few minutes without music, the engineers solved the problem and gave the Statlers the go-ahead to return. Picking up where they left off, the group dished out their snappy "This Old House" and goosed the audience with their light-heartedness. By the time they exited, after having grown "us a new eyebrow" through all the waiting, as one of the Statlers put it, the crowd was primed.

Cherry reappeared. "We're ready to do the record session. Are you ready?" Cheers. "Now I need your help. When John comes out he will say— which will be recorded—'Hi there, I'm Johnny Cash.' When he says that then you respond. Don't respond to him walking out. Welcome him after he says 'Johnny Cash.' I'll have my hands up. And you just follow me. Okay? You ready?"

That was the only way to bring Cash on stage; he needed no introduction. So Cherry held up his hands, imploring silence, and Cash paced to the mic. "Hello, I'm Johnny Cash," he bellowed. "They did what he asked, nobody said a word, it was totally still," Cash later recalled. "And when I said, 'Hello I'm Johnny Cash,' that's when they reacted. Just overwhelmed me."

If there was no other introduction, there was no other opening song. Luther's gut-deep, boom-chicka-boom intro sliced through the cavern-like dining hall, cutting open a slit through which Cash's mournful voice followed: *I hear the train a 'comin/It's rollin round the bend/And I ain't seen the sun shine/Since I don't know when.*

On the outside, at the county fairs and nightclubs, they cried for "I Walk the Line." Inside, the anthem was "Folsom Prison Blues." Everybody knew it; they mouthed the lyrics as Cash sang them. It was their song, about their wretched home. When Cash dove to the low notes, he plunged into solitary, the security housing unit, grazing against the sharp metal and jagged granite on the way down. When he said that *time kept dragging on* those who felt the clumsy passage of the hours whistled their understanding. The song was Cash's pronouncement of allegiance to the men, and when it ended like toppling metal cans, the hall erupted. They identified with "Folsom," and Cash's performance of it carried him and them both through the show in rowdy partnership.

Listeners to the album when it was released a few months later heard eruptions throughout the first song; most thrilling was a shrill cry that flew up when Cash told the prisoners he'd *shot a man in Reno*. But what the record buyers heard after Cash uttered the bloody line was pure image-making, spliced-in merriment. In reality, the crowd had remained enthralled by the first glimpse and words of the black circuit rider before them, remaining so right on through the song, saving their clamorous gusts exclusively for the its conclusion.

But the album's post-production was at that moment farther from Cash's mind than Gordon Jenkins and Landsberg, Germany. In the wake of "Folsom," what Cash *was* thinking became clear. Life is rough, especially prison life; he'd show it in song, show that he understood it. Millard Dedmon had made his way to the middle of the crowd; a jazz fan, he could have been forgiven for shunning Cash's country music, but far from it, he needed no introduction to "Folsom Prison Blues" and opened himself to Cash's vibe. "His general demeanor while performing and while there on stage, just gave you the attitude that he really understood, and was, you

(above) On stage.

(opposite) From the prisoners' view. This picture later ran in a Columbia Records advertisement for *Johnny Cash at Folsom Prison*.

(Photos by Jim Marshall)

might say, empathetic, sympathetic with our position and what we were up against, dealing with having to pay that debt."

It was time for solidarity. "Busted," "Dark As a Dungeon," "I Still Miss Someone," "Cocaine Blues." "Dark As a Dungeon" grieved over life in the coal mine, but in Folsom the mine became prison. There was no distinction. The prisoners—many of whom probably thought Cash had done hard time anyway—began to see him as their own, one of the prisoners. In Cash's mind, the line between their criminal past and his brushes with the law was probably disintegrating too. Although he'd spend the rest of his life explaining that he'd never served hard time, at this stage he routinely inflated the meaning of his scattered nights in the slammer: "I speak partly from experience," Cash wrote in his liner notes to *At Folsom Prison*. "I have been behind bars a few times. Sometimes of my own volition—sometimes involuntarily. Each time, I felt the same feeling of kinship with my fellow prisoner." He wanted to be one with him, and the songs helped him do it.

Over time, *At Folsom* joined the collection of country music's relics, Jimmie Rodgers'
guitar that passed to Ernest Tubb, a few planks from the Ryman Auditorium stage.
Cash, too, was rubbed with eternal glow, securing his throne in hillbilly heaven, next to
Rodgers, Williams, and Cline. As the stature of the album and Cash grew, so grew the
myth around "Folsom Prison Blues."

Over 12 years of a music career leading up to *At Folsom*, "Folsom Prison Blues"
was, one, a bookend, his first big hit, and, two, dubious autobiography, the source of his
audience's belief that he'd wallowed in the clink. However, by the mid-1990s new
meaning shrouded "Folsom Prison Blues," much of it cultivated by the singer's association with American Recordings.

Anybody who recalls *Time*'s darkened cover photograph of O. J. Simpson in 1994
after his arrest for murder can understand American's makeover of Johnny Cash. The
record company shone the black light on Cash's image to help it tell the story *it* wanted
to tell. And that story was about a forbidding man given to fits of half-craziness, told for
young music fans who moshed in the torrent of Nine Inch Nails and the Red Hot Chili
Peppers. Out the window—like a typewriter—flew an image twenty or more so years in
the making that had replaced sin and self-destruction with country music elder states-
manship, patriotism, and Christianity. "Folsom Prison Blues," which had never dropped
out of earshot in Cash's concerts, was newly recast in the American Recordings era as
the singer's Thompson Submachine, his intimidating entrée to the landscape of gang-
sterism and spit-in-your-face unconventionalism that American Recordings used to market a lot of its music. The song's violent *shot a man in Reno* bit was linked like father
and son to the era's brutality-filled gangsta rap. "Folsom Prison Blues," at the core
always of his repertoire, now burned at the core of his new career.

By the 1990s, it had also become an American standard, known around the world,
encrusted in a million jukeboxes, on the lips of every other bar band in the country.
Established acts covered it (Merle Haggard, Jerry Lee Lewis, and others), but as much
as it was standard, it wasn't malleable to other voices as most standards are. Nobody
who has recorded the song has ever come close to making it his own; its link to Cash is
virtually unshakable. In 2002, bluesman Keb Mo tried, but he paled to the task, recoil-
ing from the haunting line and replacing it with *They said I shot a man down in
Reno/But that was just a lie*. When Brooks and Dunn tackled "Folsom Prison Blues" a
few years earlier in 1993, they turned it into a line dance, shuffling with a go-go beat
over the song's message. Only Cash's cameo toward the song's conclusion dragged it
back down to solitary confinement. His stricken voice rapped a redemptive sequel: *It's
been thirty years now/And I know I'll never leave this God-forsaken place alive/Mama's
gone but I hear her words ringin' through my head as loud as that old train whistle
cryin' out to me night after endless night/Sending a cold steel shiver through my lost
soul/I close my eyes and pray that that iron horse is bound for the promised land/And
I'll get to ride it home to glory someday.*

On the eve of Cash's American Recordings renaissance, his addendum to "Folsom
Prison Blues" sought to direct the song's message to forgiveness and redemption. But
Cash's attempt at reorientation was lost in the spray of his new label's subsequent
marketing of him and his music.

From solidarity, he moved to a little bad-assed bravado among soul mates, coughing up his first remarks: "I just want to tell you that this show is being recorded for an album release on Columbia Records, and you can't say hell or shit or anything like that.... How does that grab you, Bob?" They guffawed at Cash's mocking of his producer Johnston, who was Cash's warden that day. "They'll probably take that word out of it," he quipped as he sank down into "I Still Miss Someone," the galloping lament of lost love whose imagery of falling leaves and cold wild winds make it one of country music's most elegant songs.

On through the morning, in a place where afternoon is morning and morning is night, the prisoners took their cues, erupting at his every move, saving the need for the engineer's splicing razor. "It exploded!" said Bob Johnston many years hence. "He could have stood up there and told stories about how he was from Arkansas and used to work in the cotton fields." Cash was swaggering. In a few breaths, it was almost like he was ready to gripe about the especially low-down batch of pruno somebody had laid on him, or the women he'd dreamt about last night, or the wretched guards who rattled his cell door to wake him for morning count or who stared into his cell all night just looking for the flash of his shank or the glow of his joint. "Let it blow" was how Cash characterized the mood in 1999. "We are in the timeless now. There is no calendar inside the cafeteria today."

Standing to Cash's right as he let it blow was Marshall Grant with his electric bass, standing like a funeral director greeting the bereaved. Grant peered at the jammed room, mesmerized by the dull glow that the long lights above cast on the prisoners. If Cash was in the timeless, Grant was swimming in the macabre, snapping back to reality only as the last bar of "Busted"—the second song of the set—faded. Before him, the crowd rose like a churning, cleansing wave. "You could feel it as it went on, you could feel it after the second song. 'Hey, there's somethin' great going on here.' And the prisoners themselves had an awful lot to do with that. They drove the nails. I mean we were there, and we did our best but, boy, the prisoners were so responsive and so appreciative. And it was just fantastic.... They came to see John. And they ate him up." And Grant and the band made

(following pages)

(left) El Matador.

(right) Sun sensations.

(Photos by Jim Marshall)

Cash all the more palatable for the eating. Through the first five songs, the sound poured like cream from a pitcher. The band pulsed, Cash hummed, and the Columbia engineers captured the mixture with soft gloves.

On stage, Cash stepped like a matador, erect, his guitar a cape. He was El Cordobés, turning Folsom's tiny wooden stage into Madrid's Plaza de Toros. Torrents of applause rushed him with every violence-charged lyric. There was, in Folsom that day, a spirit of simpatico. Marty Stuart thinks God's hand alighted on him: "The guy was on fire; he had been there enough times, and he had rehearsed that prison-singer scenario, the jail-house scenario enough to really have his act down. He was cocky. He was at the top of his game. I mean he had heaven all over him. He was just twinkling.... And I've often thought about what a master showman he was because from the flick of one finger, he could've blown that place apart."

If Cash was pouring powder from his keg, the band was striking the matches. The Tennessee Three—Luther, Marshall, and drummer Fluke Holland, as well as Carl Perkins, whose guitar filled out the band's thin patches and added the spicy flourish here and there—churned out a maddening beat. Luther's and Carl's licks slashed through the murky cafeteria air, as if they were "carved in metal," as one writer later put it. The instrumentation was undoubtedly tempered inhibition, like Cash himself, an out-of-control train that never seemed to wreck. "It's like a football team or basketball team playin' on their home court, they always do better," says Grant. "And it was the same way with us in Folsom. [The prisoners] were so enthusiastic that I think all of us just did better. I mean as I listen to that album now and I listen to other things that we done that's been recorded along about that same time, there was just a little edge on everything [at Folsom]. The tempos were up a little bit and everybody was up a little bit."

Grant's observation of the band's Folsom edge has much merit, particularly when one compares the *Folsom* album to Cash's far more popular *Live at San Quentin,* recorded and released shortly after, in 1969. Considered side by side, *San Quentin* is an eraser brushing across a chalkboard while *Folsom* is jagged fingernails scraping down the slate. In the first show at Folsom (from which virtually all of the album is culled), Cash surrendered to his heart;

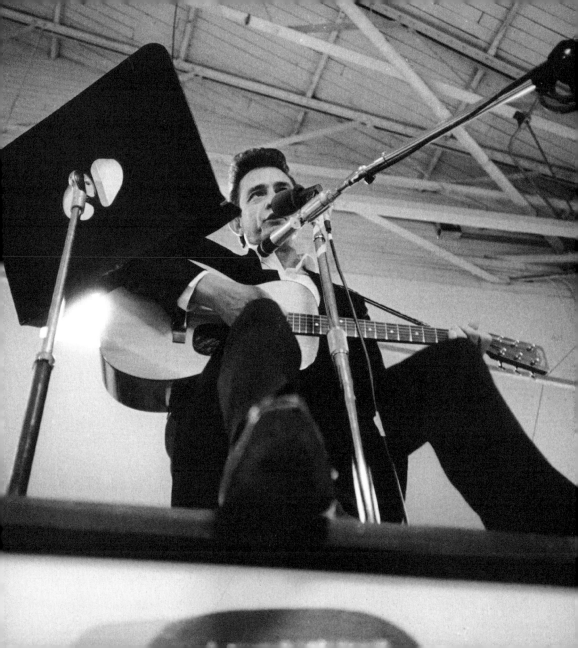

at San Quentin, Cash could have been taking cues from a director.

The second show at Folsom couldn't measure up to the first show either. By 12:40 when it began, Cash and the band, weary from the first show, were ready for bed; the edge that had cut through the morning had dulled. Only one cut from Cash's insurance policy—a performance of "Give My Love to Rose"—was dubbed onto the album.

During the first show, however, the star continued to ply his songs like a sledgehammer. On "Cocaine Blues"—the bloody ballad of unrepentant misogyny— the raucous prisoners cheered Cash the murderer as he ran from the law like a fox in the hunt, rising up at the song's every turn. He was giving all, thinking from time to time that he could have been among them. His voice teetered on collapse; the prisoners could hear the raw croaking in his throat. There was no cushion in there. It was as rough and hard as the granite quarries that lay a short distance up the American River valley on the prison grounds. He clowned through some comic relief, "25 Minutes to Go," his hanging song, but it bloodied his throat.

Cash's voice needed rest, but he pushed forward into "I'm Not in Your Town to Stay," a ballad written and recorded in 1936 by Karl Davis and Harty Taylor of the Cumberland Ridge Runners: *I'm not in your town to stay and I'll soon be on my way/I'm just here to get my baby out of jail.* But Cash slipped and forgot the words. An otherwise heartfelt rendering of a song Cash had never recorded failed to make the album. But his flub offered a seat for rest. He slowed and gave his voice respite. "You're recording this," he growled at Bob Johnston. "Ain't a damn thing happening." He dawdled, egging on the audience whose gas tank also needed filling. "Wanna be on records?" he yelped. "Go ahead and say something nice." The men squawked in glee.

Cash coughed to retrieve some moisture, some grease for the lyrics, and found a tad more respite in the extended harmonica riffs and periodic rapping in "Orange Blossom Special." After, he took a seat for "some slow ballad type songs that we wanted to do for this album, and especially for you."

Resting his long feet on the stage front and craned over his guitar, Cash showered his crowd with "slow ballad type songs" of death and imprisonment: "The Long Black Veil," "Send a Picture of Mother," and "The Wall." "I gave them a stiff shot of realism," he said later, "singing about the things they talk about, the outside, shooting, trials, families, escaping, girl friends, and coming to the end. They knew it was for them. Just them and me." But the rowdiness had died down with Cash's volleys of realism, as the prisoners seemed to be staring silently at a mirror Cash was holding up for them. One wondered just how much escape Cash was offering, what with all the ballads of misery and homicide.

And Cash appeared to recognize this, or perhaps all the while he had expected the pall to fall over the men. The sensitive showman who needed to preserve the suppleness of his audience, he lightened the mood with two strange novelties written by Jack Clement that had appeared on his *Everybody's a Nut* LP of 1966: "Dirty Old Egg-Suckin' Dog" and "Flushed from the Bathroom of Your Heart." "Flushed" was just plain weird (*At the table of your love/I got the brush off/At the Indianapolis of your heart/I lost the race*), but the prisoners indulged him anyway, rolling in joy over the corny humor.

The mournful men stuff continued to peel away with Cash's humorous ditties, but the heaviness evaporated altogether when June Carter hit the stage. (The balance of the Carter family had stayed home for this Folsom show.) As June would say in concerts everywhere (except in prisons and Billy Graham crusades), this was the "sex part" of the show. Because of just that, Cash and the band had worried that the prisoners might lay some coarseness on her. Marshall Grant: "I was afraid of what they might say and what they might do and what they might holler out, and if it'd be profanity or untasteful in any way, but that didn't happen. And maybe they had been warned before. I don't know that, but it seemed like they had because they were so well-mannered when June was out there."

If the prisoners whistled a time or two or considered her slender legs, who could blame them? June waltzed on stage in an angel's glow. Adorned conservatively in a dark suit, chestnut hair falling lightly on her shoulders, she was light streaming into a dark room. Her vision was an escape all its own. Cash flirted with her, as they launched into "Jackson," their release of

"I'm goin' to Jackson."

(Photos by Jim Marshall)

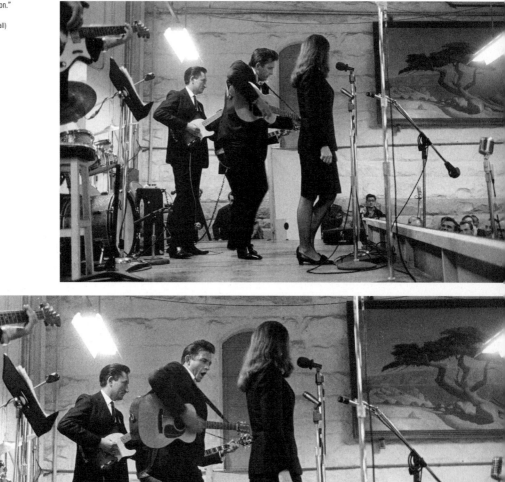

BLOW MY BLUES AWAY

BLOW MY BLUES AWAY

"We got married in fever."

(Photo by Jim Marshall)

the previous year which would be awarded a Grammy in a matter of weeks. Dueling lovers in song, theirs was comedy much sleeker and accomplished than "Flushed." Carter was the impish lover, daring her man to go to Jackson, and the audience delighted in it. She growled and did a jig, scolding her man—and the men wished she'd scold them.

In the subsiding applause after "Jackson," June addressed the men: "I enjoyed singing the song 'Jackson' with Johnny Cash. I've thought of you boys so many times having been here last year with my family [*sic*]. I really am pleased to be back and be with you." Lifted by the appreciative assembly of male admirers, she and Cash sprinted into "I Got a Woman," which was left off the final album. Remaining in the hall, though, floating like a glistening red balloon, was the possibility that June—with her looks, her flirtatiousness, her innocent humor—had nearly stolen the show.

As June handed back the stage to Cash, the show was nearing an end, and Cash searched for a landing strip. Weary from 13 rounds with Folsom, Cash's voice was flagging, but he reached for the throttle one more time and surged through "I Got Stripes," "a hard and bitter narrative of arrest and prison," commented one observer. He added the rambling "Legend of John Henry's Hammer," in which the prisoners found hilarious double entendre (*I believe this is the first time I seen the sun come up that I couldn't come up with it*). Punished by seven minutes of "John Henry," Cash peddled back to the ropes one more time, calling June back to recite one of her poems from the county fair circuit: *I went out to milk the cow one day/With my stool and bucket full of hay/I flung down my bucket, and I flopped on my stool/I said, "Be still Bossie, you stubborn ol' fool/Be still now Boss, quit jumping around/I've been out all night just a' sneakin' around"/She looked sympathetic with her eyes big and brown/And said, "Just hang on, and I'll jump up and down."*

It should have sunk like a stone in the American River, but from June's lips it was Frost; the inmates mustered a generous reaction.

Where was Cash's knockout punch, the Glen Sherley song? He needed it, but he saved it. Meandering through an obligatory rather uninspired take on Curly Putnam's "Green Green Grass of Home," the dream of the death row inmate, which Cash had never recorded in the studio, it was one too

(opposite) "Greystone Chapel."
Doing it justice.

(above) Carter and the Statlers.

(following pages)
Reading Sherley's lyrics.

(Photos by Jim Marshall)

many prison songs over the line. Did the prisoners really need so many reminders of their bleak circumstance?

Finally, he reared back and unfurled "Greystone Chapel." "This next song was written by a man right here in Folsom Prison, and last night was the first time I've ever sung this song. And we may be a little rough on it today. We may have to do it twice. We'll definitely do it again on our next show in order to try to get a new recording of it because it is new and it may be released as a single record out of the album, I'm not sure. Anyway ... this song was written by our friend Glen Sherley." The men—a little rough feeling themselves—hoisted a cheer. He looked down at Sherley: "Hope we do your song justice, Glen." He looked at his band: "What key do we do it in?"

Sufficiently oriented and with June Carter and the Statlers crooning behind, Cash straddled Sherley's unwieldy ballad. *There's a greystone chapel here in Folsom/A house of worship in this den of sin.* When Cash uttered these lines, the applause cracked up from the floor like unexpected thunder. Throughout the show the reaction had not been so decisive, so serious. But somehow "Greystone" commented on their plight like no other song that day had, not even "Folsom Prison Blues." It was a symbol of Cash's bond with convicts and the possibility of redemption—and it remained so. *You wouldn't think that God had a place here at Folsom/But he saved the soul of many lost men.*

In the raining applause, Cash reached down to shake Sherley's hand before hustling back to the kitchen area. The second show in two hours loomed. At some point near their utilitarian backstage, a prisoner-worker broke the rules and approached him. "Johnny," he called.

BLOW MY BLUES AWAY

(above) It's a wrap. Sherley enters Cash's backstage.

(left) Inmate Sherley with Cherry and Cash.

(Photos by Jim Marshall)

117

A guard moved to restrain the man, but the singer waved him away. "The guard let him have one question," Cash later recalled. "You know so 'n' so back in Arkansas?' 'Never heard the name,' I said. 'He said he knew you,' the kid said, and the guard pushed him back. He broke the rules just trying to make a country boy connection."

Another prisoner got closer once they got backstage. He extended his sinewy tattooed arm and Cash seized it. It was Glen Sherley again. The two laughed and chatted easily before the next show. "[He] may have been a prisoner," recalls Marshall Grant, "but this is the happiest man I've ever seen in my life when they allowed him to come backstage. It had to be the biggest day in his life because he liked to have died when John did 'Greystone Chapel.'" According to Grant, Sherley saw from the beginning that using his song to wrangle a meeting with Cash could be the vehicle to ride out of Folsom. "His plan was to see if he could make a mark somehow with John, and maybe somehow someway get out.... Glen told me this himself." The scheme would prove successful.

The second show proved superfluous insurance. Bob Johnston cut from it Johnny's "Give My Love to Rose" and spliced it into the album, and, to convey the air of prison, he transported a few announcements that had thundered over the P.A. system calling prisoners away from the show. The associate warden's brief recognition ceremony at the conclusion of the final show also magically drifted to the first show and onto the album. Most of the second outing, though, paled next to the first show. Cash sagged, although the second corps of prisoners yearned to dance and make merry with him. Technical problems as well, overmodulation perhaps, muddied the sound from time to time, consigning the second show to Columbia's vaults.

Leaving Sherley and Dedmon and 2,000 prisoners, he and June were escorted outside, where they strolled unencumbered to the prison bus waiting to carry them to the gates. "When you comin' back?" an inmate shouted.

"Next year," replied Cash.

They had shed the long, leather coats and grimaces of the morning. Smiling now, they skipped past the lines of prisoners and staff who watched them closely. If the morning had been a funeral procession, the afternoon was a wedding march. A few more pictures for Jim Marshall, a farewell to Bob Johnston and his hosts, and then, on a swell of triumph, he was gone. "It was a great day," declares Grant. "There's no question about that: a great, great, great day."

As Cash pulled away, blue skies stretched far beyond the walls, beyond the American River, to San Francisco maybe. Above the city of deviant souls, warm winter light shone down.

Out to the day.

(Photo by Jim Marshall)

(opposite) Warm winter light shone down.

(above) A wedding march?

(near left) "How's that grab you, Bob?"

(following pages) Inside the prison bus to the outside.

(Photos by Jim Marshall)

GOOD BOY

*If you've got an image, you sell records on the image, if you see what I mean, and
you can always rely on a following.* — Mick Jagger

0004

While Bob Johnston and his engineer took razor and tape to the
Folsom tapes, paring the two shows into one sixteen-song set and begrudg-
ingly cutting or bleeping out Cash's raw language, the Johnny Cash touring
show hit the road in mid-January on a typically rigorous month-long swing
through the mid-South, the Northeast, and Canada. When he was off the
road in the weeks and months after Folsom and before the scheduled late-
May album release of the concert, his days were no less hectic: Memphis
and Dyess splashed homecoming fetes on Cash; he and June accepted a
country and western Grammy in Nashville for their duet "Jackson"; he
signed a new Columbia contract at a ceremony with CBS Records chief
Clive Davis (who was satisfied, apparently, that the Folsom concert had not

One more for the road.

(Photo by Jim Marshall)

killed the singer's career); and he journeyed to Israel to breathe the air of Christ, a pilgrimage documented in his *Holy Land* album of late 1968. However, amid the push and pull of Cash's career there was no bigger event than his marriage to June Carter. He had proposed on stage during a February show in London, Ontario, and within a month, they married in Franklin, Kentucky. The union would prove to be a fort in which Cash took refuge from his ever-fluctuating war against drugs and weakness: "What June did for me was post signs along the way, lift me up when I was weak, encourage me when I was discouraged, and love me when I felt alone and unlovable."

Sweet moments with his new wife—the sojourn to Israel was a working honeymoon—and relentless travel at home and abroad likely distracted Cash from the spring release of *At Folsom,* but he wasn't alone in preoccupation: Columbia Records appeared to be looking the other way, too. With little mass market fanfare, the album slipped unobtrusively into America's record stores.

Readied in four months, nobody at Columbia believed the company could turn *Folsom* into a blockbuster; the possibility appears never to have crossed anybody's mind. "For me to tell you that Columbia Records did some phenomenal thing [to fire up sales] would not be true," said Joe Casey, a regional promotion man in Atlanta at the time. "We just started working it." The album—which ultimately sold millions—was absent from the company's summer portfolio ads (which made room for far less dynamic artists such as Jimmy Dean, Gale Garnett, Stonewall Jackson, and Jim Nabors), and no advance advertising appeared in the trade press, a sure sign of modest expectations. Columbia shipped advance copies to reviewers, but in the ears of mass market America only a faint buzz encircled the album release as well as its first (and only) single "Folsom Prison Blues," which threatened to flop if too many people assumed it was just a rerelease of the 1955 Sun classic.

Despite *Folsom*'s quiet release, Columbia could hardly be accused of blind neglect. The recent success of "Rosanna's Going Wild" notwithstanding, few in the company had any reason to expect a smash hit from Cash.

X

COLUMBIA RECORDING STUDIO
6121 SUNSET BLVD.
HOLLYWOOD, 28, CALIFORNIA

Date 1/13/68

Client # 150

Program Johnny Cash
Folsom   Co. Engr. Bob Breault   Re. Engr. Bill Brittain

Job No. _____ Reel No. 1A

TAPE SPEED: # 15

☐ MONO ☐ TWO TR ☐ THREE TR.
☑ FOUR TR ☐ EIGHT TR

	TITLE	TAKE NO.	CODE	TAKE NO.	CODE	TAKE NO.	CODE	TIME
	TONES 1re 10re 50cy							
1	— ANNONCER —							
2	BLUE SUEDE SHOES (CARL PERKINS)							2:20
3	THIS OLD HOUSE (STATLER BROS)							1:27
4	FLOWERS ON THE WALL (STATLER BROS)							2:05
5	THIS OLD HOUSE							1:30
NCO98435 6	FOLSOM PRISON (JOHNNY CASH)							2:30
NCO 98436 7	I'M BUSTED " "							1:10
98437 ✓ 8	DARK AS A DUNGEON " "							2:35
98438 9	BLUE EYES (I STILL MISS SOMEONE) "							2:35
98439 ✓ 10	COCAINE SONG " BITCH "							2:35
98440 11	25 MINUTES TO GO " "							2:55
98441 ✓ 12	I'M NOT IN YOUR TOWN TO STAY " "							1:40
98442 13	ORANGE BLOSSOM SPECIAL " "							?
98443 14	NOBODY KNOWS BUT ME " (LONG BLACK VEIL)							8:00
98444 15	SEND A PICTURE OF MOTHER " "							?
98445 16	STARING AT THE WALL " "							1:30
98446 17	EGG SUCKING DOG " "							1:05
98447 18	BACK DOOR OF YOUR LIFE " "							?

1st

SHOW

TAPE DISPOSITION: ☐ FILE   ☐ HOLD   ☐ PICK UP   ☐ SHIP

√ False Start   B Long False Start   C Complete Take   (C) Master

Date **1/13/68**

Client **JOHNSTON**

Program **Johnny Cash** Co. Engr **Bob Breault** Re. Engr **Bill Britain**

Studio **FOLSOM**

COLUMBIA RECORDING STUDIO
6121 SUNSET BLVD.
HOLLYWOOD, 28, CALIFORNIA

Job No. _____ Reel No. **2A**

TAPE SPEED: **#15**

☐ MONO ☐ TWO TR ☐ THREE TR.
☑ FOUR TR ☐ EIGHT TR

MASTER NO.		TITLE	TAKE NO.	CODE	TAKE NO.	CODE	TAKE NO.	CODE	TIME
		— OVERLAP ON 2B —							1³⁰
NCO 98448	1	JOE BEAM (Johnny Cash)							?
98449	2	JACKSON (June Carter Johnny)							245
98450	3	~~I~~ I GOT A WOMAN (" " ")							6³⁰
98451	4	JOHN HENRY (Johnny Cash)							?
—	5	POEM (June Carter)							230
98452	6	GREEN GREEN GRASS (Johnny Cash)							240
98~~453~~	7	INSIDE THE WALLS (Johnny Cash)							
	8	" " " REPEAT END							
	9	END SHOW #1							

1st Show
TO END

TAPE DISPOSITION: ☐ FILE   ☐ HOLD   ☐ PICK UP   ☐ SHIP

√ False Start   B Long False Start   C Complete Take   Ⓒ Master

CR 724 (REV. 8/66)

COLUMBIA RECORDING STUDIO
6121 SUNSET BLVD.
HOLLYWOOD, 28, CALIFORNIA

Date 1/13/68

Client Johnston

Program Johnny Cash   Co. Engr. Bob Breault   Re. Engr. Bill Britian

Studio Folsom

Job No. ____   Reel No. 3-A

TAPE SPEED: #15

☐ MONO   ☐ TWO TR   ☐ THREE TR.
☑ FOUR TR   ☐ EIGHT TR

MASTER NO.		TITLE		TAKE NO.	CODE	TAKE NO.	CODE	TAKE NO.	CODE	TIME
		SHOW #2 BEGIN.								
	1.	WARM UP - BY BAND -								
	2.	ANNOUNCER								2:30
	3.	MATCHBOX HOLE IN MY CLOTHES (CARL PERKINS)								1:45
	4.	BLUE SUEDE SHOES	" "							1:55
	5.	CAN'T HAVE YOUR CAKE (STATLER BROS								?
	6.	AIN'T GOT TIME	" "							2:00
	7.	FLOWERS ON THE WALL	" "							?
	8.	HOW GREAT THOU ART	" "							2:40
NC098435	9.	FOLSOM PRISON (JOHNNY CASH)								1:15
98436	10.	I'M BUSTED	" "							2:45
98437	11.	DARK DUNGEON	" "							2:35
98439	12	COCAINE	" "							2:35
98440	13	25 MINUTES TO GO	" "							3:05
98442	14	ORANGE BLOSSOM SPECIAL	" "							6:35
98451	15	JOHN HENRY	" "							

2nd SHOW

TAPE DISPOSITION: ☐ FILE   ☐ HOLD   ☐ PICK UP   ☐ SHIP

√ False Start   B Long False Start   C Complete Take   Ⓒ Master

CR 724 (REV. 8/66)

COLUMBIA RECORDING STUDIO
6121 SUNSET BLVD.
HOLLYWOOD, 28, CALIFORNIA

Date 1/13/68

Client Johnston

Program Johnny Cash

Studio Folsom Co. Engr Bob Breault Re. Engr Bill Britain

Job No. ___ Reel No. 4A

TAPE SPEED: # 15

- [ ] MONO
- [ ] TWO TR
- [ ] THREE TR.
- [x] FOUR TR
- [ ] EIGHT TR

MASTER NO.	TITLE	TAKE NO.	CODE	TAKE NO.	CODE	TAKE NO.	CODE	TIME
	OVERLAP ON 3B							
NCO 98455	1. Give My Love To Rose (June + Johnny)							2.00
98446	2. Egg Sucking Dog (Johnny Cash)							3.00
98447	3. Back Door Of Your Life " "							2.45
98448	4. Joe Bean " "							1.25
98449	5. Jackson (June + Johnny)							2.25
98456	6. Big Mouth Woman " " "							2.05
98457	7. I Got Stripes (Johnny Cash)							1.25
98452	8. Green Green Grass " "							?
98454	9. Grey Stone Prison " "							2.45
	10. " " " Repeat							2.45

2nd SHOW
To BMI

TAPE DISPOSITION:
- [ ] FILE
- [ ] HOLD
- [ ] PICK UP
- [ ] SHIP

√ False Start   B Long False Start   C Complete Take   Ⓒ Master

CR 724 (REV. 8/66)

In the years since his last big hit in 1964, the company had redirected its marketing and promotion efforts towards artists who could deliver more return on investment: Bob Dylan, Barbra Streisand, Simon and Garfunkel, and even Ray Price and Marty Robbins on the country side. The label cranked out something like 30 albums and 40 singles per month, and, as its former vice president for marketing Wornall Farr explains, only the releases with legs to hurdle into the big-selling arena got big promotional dollars: "We never had what we thought was enough money to promote the whole [roster] properly. So you had to then allocate based on the actual record sales that were coming in at a certain point. The other thing ... was we supported a very large classical catalog, just as RCA did. A lot of promotional money had to be devoted to that, and it was basically siphoning money out of the pop area in order to subsidize it. So it was a constant push and pull for advertising funds, and a push and pull from the hottest artist that you would sign with certain promises." In the spring of 1968 there were no promises due Cash from Farr or anybody else at Columbia; he was not among Columbia's big hurdlers. "He wasn't considered a sure bet, that's for sure," adds Tom Noonan, Columbia's national promotion manager at the time.

Even in the best of times—when a "Ring of Fire" or an "Understand Your Man" broke out—finding promotion dollars for country artists was like searching for a baseball in the ivy. Most country artists of the day and their managers—no matter their label affiliation—griped about the dearth of promotional attention. Johnny Cash and his roster mates at Columbia were no exception. Country—with its modest sales—was decidedly not king. "It wasn't viewed with a lot of respect," says Farr. To many at Columbia, Nashville sounds were a whiskey still off in the woods, a sure enough moneymaker but one you'd think twice about being around. Nashville A&R man and Cash producer Frank Jones heard the ambivalence always, but never as loudly as in the mid-1960s when he answered a call from Columbia-New York's marketing people:

Columbia: "Frank, we have a convention coming up, you know that?"
Jones: "Yeah, I'm aware of it."

Columbia: "Well, how would you like to present Johnny Horton with a gold record on stage?"

Jones: "No, I don't think so."

Columbia: "Why not?"

Jones: "He's dead. He's been dead for five years."

Columbia: "Oh."

How could *Folsom* charge up the charts given the company's lack of faith in country music and Cash's unlikely potential? And what about the landmines that the unpredictable singer himself scattered about? Columbia, which had not considered dropping Cash even in his darkest drug-addled days, found it difficult to use Cash himself on what promotional efforts it did expend on his records. If the label arranged radio station visits, meetings with important distributors, or invited bigwigs to concerts to impress them, Wornell Farr observed that the label never knew if Cash would engage the moment, stumble through it, or just plain go AWOL. "So you were never really sure just what his mood was going to be or how he was going to get up on the stage and get back down off of it. It worried us considerably because we had no control over it. We simply had to live with it." In promotion, as in other facets of his career, Cash could be his own worst enemy.

Tom Noonan—who would move to Motown Records in late 1968 some months after *Folsom's* release—knew, like Farr, that Cash wasn't the sharpest public relations tool in the shed, learning as much one night in Miami when the Johnny Cash show pulled into town just as Noonan was convening a sales conference there. Naturally, recalls Noonan, somebody thought a meeting with Cash would somehow buoy the sales staff. "After dinner we all got in cabs or whatever and we went to Miami Auditorium where Cash was performing. He had a packed audience.... So we went backstage and, sure enough, Cash was there. And Cash was kind of high. I'll never forget this, he had his thumb in the hottest cup of coffee you'd ever seen. Smoke was coming out of it, and his thumb was in the coffee.... He'd take up the cup to his lips and just tilt it. He never felt that." One by one, Cash greeted the awed and befuddled reps, his thumb submerged through every handshake.

Eschewing the expensive mass market promotion route for *At Folsom,* the company earnestly plugged the album in the underground media where disc jockeys, editors, and columnists flogged an anti-establishment agenda. Columbia placed ads and courted reviews in alternative periodicals such as *The Seed* (Chicago), *The Washington Free Press* (Washington, D.C.), and *The Village Voice* (New York), which, in turn, encouraged airplay on underground radio, the rebellious format that was the soundtrack for underground journalism's anti-government, free-sex, back-to-nature agenda. The electronic calliope on the radio airwaves sprouted from San Francisco where former AM disc jockey Tom Donahue, a refugee from the payola-scorched East Coast, snubbed rigid musical formats to feature whatever sounded good to him, commercial or non-commerical, whether it be rock, folk, blues, jazz, or classical. In its variety, there was rebellion that attracted the Monterey generation sick of AM radio's constant rotation of top 40 hits. Taking Donahue's baton, the *Los Angeles Times'* Tom Nolan suggested it was more than escape from top 40: "It has something to do with the excitement people feel at a given moment about given performers and their creations; and ... usually this excitement is over the things that are vital and regenerating to the scene at the moment."

Stations in markets such as Salt Lake City, Dallas, Boston, Philadelphia, Rochester, Cincinnati, and Detroit followed San Francisco's example, dedicating chunks of their broadcast day, if not the entire day, to the kaleidoscopic underground playlist. Anything could happen in the underground: Moby Grape's "Omaha" might be followed by a Fugs' album cut followed by a deejay's poem read over Country Joe and the Fish instrumentals followed by an unauthorized twenty-minute deejay edit of Jimi Hendrix's "Purple Haze." The music could be now, and it could be then, digging back through the ages for Miles Davis, John Coltrane, Buddy Holly, Little Richard, and Bill Haley. No Frankie Avalon or Bobby Vee, thank you.

Underground disc jockeys—like their brothers and sisters in the press—violated any convention in sight, playing records laced with obscenities, avoiding commercials, and showing up behind the microphones high and mellow, in contrast to their perky Top 40 counterparts. Peter C.

Cavanaugh, of WTAC in Detroit—one of the few AM stations that aired underground—routinely arrived "ripped" for his nighttime underground shift, and as consciousness allowed, cooled his disc jockey patter for his hip audience. "I pulled my vocal pitch 'down' rather than 'up.' Not a hint of 'commercial hype' was left in any information conveyed. My delivery slowed to an almost hesitant semi-crawl. I was as coooooooool as the rock was hot. The whole idea was to act as juxtaposition to the music, and to convey the feeling of being sturdy, but definitely stoned."

Although few country marketing reps stopped to visit jocks of Cavanaugh's persuasion, the emerging scene personified by Cavanaugh, Richard Goldstein of *The Village Voice,* and Jann Wenner of *Rolling Stone* attracted Columbia's eyes when it plotted *Folsom's* release. Within days of Cash's new release, the album drew applause, the *Voice* proclaiming it a "deeply moving 'live' concert," and *Rolling Stone* dubbing it "one of his very best." The underground consumer heard the clapping.

Released from the gate to the care of underground media, the single "Folsom Prison Blues" rumbled onto the *Billboard* country charts. It was June 1, 1968.

Anybody could have predicted it; nary a Cash single failed to hit country. However, almost nobody could have imagined the single's debut on the

The original 45 RPM single of "Folsom Prison Blues" on Columbia, released in 1968.

pop charts a week earlier, on May 25. Defying Columbia's modest expectations, "Folsom" was poised to join "Ring of Fire" and "I Walk the Line" among the list of Cash's hottest sellers. But then the record, and the nation, took a surprise blow. Just as quickly as the pop and country disc jockeys and their program directors had embraced the 45 rpm single, they laid the record aside, nearly killing the album sales that often come on the heels of a best-selling single. On June 5, 1968, a disgruntled Palestinian, Sirhan Bishara Sirhan, gunned down Robert F. Kennedy in Los Angeles, bewildering (right) *Johnny Cash at Folsom Prison*, released in May 1968.

(far right) Spanish 45 RPM release of "Folsom Prison Blues," 1968.

JOHNNY CASH
AT FOLSOM PRISON

JOHNNY CASH
FOLSOM PRISON BLUES
THE FOLK SINGER

Folsom Prison Blues
Orange Blossom Special
The Long Black Veil
Jackson
(With June Carter)
Green, Green Grass of Home
I Got Stripes
Dirty Old Egg-sucking Dog
The Wall
25 Minutes to Go
Dark as the Dungeon
I Still Miss Someone
Cocaine Blues
Send a Picture of Mother
Give My Love to Rose
(With June Carter)
Flushed From the Bathroom of Your Heart

a country already traumatized by Martin Luther King, Jr.'s assassination two months earlier and the Vietnam war's televised procession of body bags. Radio stations guessed that listeners couldn't stomach "Folsom's" grisly *shot a man in Reno* line and the gleeful, though dubbed-in, outburst of the prisoners that accompanied it, so they pulled it from rotation.

The record's momentum flagging, Columbia scrambled to reinvigorate it. Executives ordered Bob Johnston to cut the offensive line from the radio edit and reship it to stations. Johnston made the changes and shipped the new version to Pitman, New Jersey, where Columbia pressed its disc jockey records (the retail records went unchanged). But Cash blanched. *Why mess*

Ready to go, with his ill-fitting gift from the associate warden.

(Photo by Jim Marshall)

with my song? In response, Clive Davis put promotion manager Tom Noonan on the job. "Tom, you're close to Cash," Noonan recalls his boss saying. "Call him up and tell him that we're going to edit that line out of that cut. He's resisting the idea totally." From his home in Matawan, New Jersey, Noonan dialed the singer whom he thought was just a little spooky. Thumb in coffee notwithstanding, Noonan found it both odd and amusing that Cash referred to "Johnny Cash" in the third person. Was Cash a split personality or was he merely distancing himself from the commodity that Johnny Cash was? In any case, he and Noonan discussed in earnest what to do about the "Johnny Cash" record. "It took a lot of begging and pleading with him for about an hour on the phone. I was on the phone for maybe 45 minutes to an hour pleading with him to let me edit this record. He didn't want it to be edited. I said, 'John, you have to let me edit this record because we're off the air. We want to get back on the air.' And I kept pleading with him." Throughout the conversation, Noonan's wife cued and re-cued the original and edited versions while Noonan held the phone to the speaker so Cash could compare the two. Finally, Cash relented, and a few thousand fresh white-labeled deejay copies rolled out of Pitman to stations across the country.

As late spring became summer, the album and single reawakened, leaping up the pop and country charts and spurring Columbia to hastily assemble a few ads for the trade press. One—a front page cube in *Billboard* which was designed to look like a news photo and caption—read, "Johnny is being discovered everywhere from Underground to Top 40, and the new album, 'Johnny Cash At Folsom Prison,' with its single, is naturally headed for the top too." (Columbia reserved such cubes for last minute plugs.) By late June, *At Folsom* hit #84 on the pop charts where it mingled with a diverse assortment of albums such as *There Is* by the Dells, *The Beat Goes On* by Vanilla Fudge, *Easy* by Nancy Wilson, and the *Dr. Doolittle* soundtrack. *At Folsom* was well on the way to peaking at #13. An ascent so dramatic on the pop album charts was unprecedented in Cash's career, and rare among all country artists. Only a handful of country albums had climbed so high (including various dynamic outings by Glen Campbell, Eddy Arnold's *My World* of 1965, and Bobbie Gentry's *Ode to Billie Joe* of 1967).

In drilling into the underground, Columbia had struck a tunnel to pop sales. "Underground was appealing to the kids of those days, the hippies ...," says Tom Noonan. "Whatever underground was playing, they were buying like crazy, so we had to play to that, which we did." Columbia offered up few acts in 1968 that appealed to the underground—Dylan, Pete Seeger, Moby Grape—so when the stations picked up *Folsom,* Columbia pounced, realizing finally that Cash and the prisoner's vehemence (trumped up as it was by studio tricks and Hugh Cherry's entreaties) resonated with a generation that sought freedom through the unconventional. "That album appealed to the underground because of the nature of it," says Noonan. "Because it was made in a prison and the prison was in California, and that's where

The critical reaction to *Johnny Cash At Folsom Prison* from the mainstream and underground media coalesced in near unanimity by mid-summer of 1968, cheering the album and overshadowing almost every other current album release. There were no dissenting reviews.

The underground press—including *The Village Voice* and *Rolling Stone*—sensed the album's bold message and unwrought feel before mainstream journalists pulled their heads from the sand. No surprise there. But Marshall Grant credits the public with climbing *Mt. Folsom* first. "They're the ones that recognized it," admits Marshall Grant. "We didn't. I can't say that we were all that proud of this album; it was an exciting album, as we realized later. We listened to it a few times and, well, we released it. But if you listen to it, it's pretty rough. The mix on the album is as good as you could expect as far as instrumentation is concerned and all the voices and everything. But it's real rough. But this roughness made it real. And it made it part of the chemistry. The country music fan of the world is the one that discovered it was a success. They're the ones that did it; it wasn't us. We just recorded it."

If the fans ignited *Folsom's* explosive dash from the blocks, music writers maintained its gazelle-like pace with their adoring reviews:

"Cash's voice is as thick and gritty as ever, but filled with the kind of emotionalism you seldom find in rock (for all the hue and cry about passionate intensity, white pop singers don't often let go, do they?). His songs are simple and sentimental, his message clear.... The feeling of hopelessness—even amid the cheers and whistles—is overwhelming. You come away drained, as the record fades out to the sound of men booing their warden, and a guard's gentle, but deadly warning, 'Easy now.' Talk about magical mystery tours."

—Richard Goldstein, *The Village Voice*, June 6, 1968

"All the excitement of Cash's recent appearance at Folsom Prison is captured in one of the year's best albums. From the opening 'Folsom Prison Blues' to the closing 'Greystone Chapel,' Cash is at his dynamic best in this 'live' offering of 16 songs."

—Robert Hilburn, *Los Angeles Times*, June 16, 1968

"This new album ... is Johnny Cash at his best.... Beginning with 'Folsom Prison Blues,' the album is a virtual goldmine of some of the oldest songs in country music."

—Tom Henry, *Washington Free Press*, June 24-July 3, 1968

underground broke from." Rumors of Cash's supposed time in the pen stirred the market's interest as well, and Columbia did little to discourage the talk, actually fanning the wild rumors in its underground press ads: "He's been in prison before," read the melodramatic advertising copy. "Not always on a visit." If the hyped prison stories sold records, the Columbia marketing and promotion people let them fly.

In mid-July, as the album and the single topped the country charts,

"Now, out of Johnny Cash's underground comes country music's answer to that latest of pop vogues, the album with a theme, an LP programmed to sound like a show with a unity rather than a collection of songs.... Johnny Cash sings these songs with the deep baritone conviction of someone who has grown up believing he is one of the people that these songs are about."

—Alfred G. Aronowitz, *Life*, August 16, 1968

"The Folsom album seems to appeal to a wider, more diverse audience than anything else he has ever done; it ranks among the top choices of the bestseller charts not only for country music but also for pop, and it has received glowing reviews in the underground rock publications.... In fact, the album stands as a timely symbol of the growing infusion of country sounds into the U.S. pop mainstream."

—*Time*, August 30, 1968

"Every cut is special in its own way, but it is difficult not to read also the album's fascinating sociological messages."

—Annie Fisher, *The Village Voice*, October 17, 1968

"Good basic performance from America's great country and western artists, recorded 'live' at Folsom Prison. Cash achieves an immediate, warm rapport with his convict audience."

—Donald Heckman, *American Record Guide,* December 1968

"For not only is the album a live performance; it is also an album structured as an aural experience for us: it builds its own gestalt which is not exactly the same as if we were present. And herein lies the remarkable quality of this live recording over most others. We don't have to excuse the quality of the recording or the rehash of old hits or medleys as we do in nearly all live-performance recordings. Every song and response here fits into a total impression."

—Frederick E. Danker, *Sing Out!,* September/October 1969

while topping out on the pop side at #13 and #32, respectively, the mass media began to pick up the underground's buzz, scrutinizing Cash and tracking his album's trajectory. They wrote about the singer as if he were a real prisoner made good. Cash, a recovering drug addict, maybe an ex-con, in prison, playing the tough guy in front of 1,000 pent-up men; what record promoter or editor could ignore the angle? It was 1960s rebellion, a sidebar to the street battles between the SDS and Richard Daley's police outside the 1968 Democratic convention. Cash was the disgruntled vandal, the marginalized arsonist, stalking through Folsom Prison to settle old scores, if not to rip out the building's iron bars one by one. Cash's swearing—his bleeped out "shits" and "damns"—salted his ruddy image. He uttered them unconsciously it seemed; there was, he told journalist Dorothy Gallagher, just no other way to speak to his prison audiences. "They finally got somebody singin' it to them just the way it is.... They want me to say 'bitch' and 'bastard.' Profanity is a vital, big part of a prisoner's vocabulary. If I didn't use it, they'd think I was a pantywaist."

In August, *Life* was among the first publications to flog the quasi-criminal image conceived at Folsom. Skimming Cash from the rest of country music's milk as writers had been wont to do since the singer met Dylan, the magazine's Al Aronowitz painted an outlaw, "a face that might have been ripped off a wanted poster, a voice that sounds as though it's coming through a bandanna mask." And Aronowitz's colleagues followed him, flocking to this image like chickens to the feed. Their Cash was a mean dude, with an unfeigned contempt for the law. Few bothered to burrow below the prison showman veneer to mention his marriage to June, his slow recovery from drugs, or the days he'd just spent in Israel seeking the footsteps of Christ. The media clatter presaged Cash's American years of the 1990s, when reporters ran slack-jawed to the singer's newly polished black image.

As sales of *Folsom* reached 300,000 in August, Cash's forbidding visage grew unnaturally swollen. *Time* magazine contributed to the bloat: "Cash, lean and tough looking at 36, sings with granite conviction and mordant wit about sadness, pain, loneliness and hard luck." Sure, Cash put forth stark countenance, but the writer either forgot or ignored, or just didn't know that Cash sang love songs, novelties, and historical ballads, and that occasionally he even smiled, but because he had been granite at Folsom, he was granite always. Cash would only become more human to the public, more multi-dimensional, when *Folsom*'s flame cooled. As Elvis observed a few years later, "The image is one thing. The man is another." Cash could relate.

But the feverish Cash-image exploitation alone doesn't account entirely for the album's appeal in the underground and above and below: The location of the show, the place, put the album in more than a few hands. Even with its splices here and there, *At Folsom* revealed prison in a form akin to cinema vérité, more realistically than any book or B-grade feature film, such as *Inside the Walls of Folsom*. Listeners heard tumbling from their hi-fi speakers the steely clattering of prison doors, the cathartic cries of 1,000 imprisoned men. It was hard to listen to *Folsom* without hearing the rigid, cold place it was—even if Cash was warming it just for a while: metal on metal echoing through the lost caverns, the prisoners' reluctant march out of the cafeteria after the show; the jingling keys that opened the doors that led to cage after cage, and the sterile announcements that punctuated the show, stolidly summoning men by their surnames and numbers ("Duffy, number 907, custody office").

The place also renewed many of Cash's songs. As he yanked them from his repertoire like a railroad bull collaring freeloading hobos, the Folsom atmosphere transformed them and gave them new appeal. "Folsom Prison Blues," obviously, was never so wicked, just as "I Still Miss Someone" was never so lonely as Cash's lyrics echoed off the prison's desolate walls. Songs about regret and longing and songs that lamented back-breaking labor and poverty became songs of imprisonment, underscoring for listeners what Cash already knew too well: that you don't have to be in prison to be imprisoned.

In October, as *At Folsom* was certified gold, signifying sales of 500,000, it was apparent that the underground exposure had triggered spending among audiences who had rarely if ever purchased Cash discs. Certainly, Cash's base in the country audience composed in part the foundation of *At Folsom's* ascent; they had known him and faithfully bought his records since 1956 and "I Walk the Line." In contrast, though, the underground audience (largely composed of folk and rock fans) who sought the album on the shelves of Village Oldies in Manhattan and Jack's Record Cellar in San Francisco had undoubtedly known him and admired him. However, they had seen little reason to buy his records; after all, he *was* just a country artist.

But the endorsement of underground radio and, perhaps more important, his ongoing and visible association with Bob Dylan and folk music helped convert many to Cash. After their public meeting and Cash's recording of "Don't Think Twice It's Alright," "It Ain't Me Babe," and "Mama You've Been on My Mind" on his 1965 LP *Orange Blossom Special,* a curiosity about Cash grew among those who would otherwise have overlooked him. And then the relationship collected into sharper focus when Dylan hit Nashville in the winter of 1966 to record the classic *Blonde on Blonde* and again in the fall of 1967 to work on *John Wesley Harding,* sojourns—whatever their impetus—that did nothing to hurt Cash's image among the folk and rock people.

His image grew more lustrous among the curious when, on the eve of *At Folsom*'s release, the new rock tabloid *Rolling Stone* seized the notion that Cash was molding Dylan, spotlighting their relationship in black and white and legitimating theories about Cash's influence on Dylan. Publisher Jann Wenner wrote that Cash's "heartfelt" and "soulfull" style was rubbing off on the younger singer. He saw a blood pact between the two rising from Cash's presentation of his guitar to Dylan at Newport in 1964, and, with no apparent hesitation, placed the two on one plane: "They share the same tradition, they are good friends, and the work of each can tell you about the work of the other." Wenner's article, printed in May of 1968, rolled out on the presses just one month after the magazine had run a large picture of Dylan performing at Carnegie Hall under the upper-cased headline: "THE NEW BOB DYLAN: A LITTLE LIKE JOHNNY CASH?"

It and Columbia's marketing in the underground press were a mass invitation to check out Cash's music, and when *At Folsom* appeared on its antiestablishment horse, the underground audience accepted a ride. *At Folsom* was their reason to finally invest in him. Its solidarity with the prisoners spoke the language of the 1960s, its forlorn ballads and criminal "Folsom Prison Blues" seeming to be the essence of rock music.

Folsom also parachuted Cash into the thick of the burgeoning country-rock scene, which was really Cash's domain anyway. One need only to gently scratch the skin of late 1960s country rockers such as the Flying Burrito Brothers, the Byrds, and the Buffalo Springfield to find the blood of Johnny Cash. Going back almost 15 years, many of his Sun recordings were as torpid as the most fiery rock and roll of the day, with its Jagger-like swagger, throbbing backbeat, jarring electric guitar. But Cash's music was so scarred, so pocked, it just wasn't pretty enough to be lumped with the rock and roll of the 1950s, so it was labeled country, product for the dirt farmers and oil-stained truck drivers. *Folsom* translated Cash's rocking Memphis inclinations for the rockers of the late 1960s, country or otherwise.

Over the next thirty-five years, *Folsom's* sales reached platinum and then multi-platinum levels. One of pop music's essential albums, it remains in print to this day.

Yet over the years—despite the sales and the stature in popular music that it granted—its social statement, which had so much to do with its appeal, faded. *Folsom* clearly represented a turning point for country music and for Johnny Cash. And it forged a badge of authority in Cash's condemnation of imprisonment. But as a relevant social declaration in the Age of Aquarius, *Folsom* has proven to be a leaky jug, which is surprising in light of the intense interest in the album in 1968 and in Cash as a spokesperson immediately post-Folsom (Tom Dearmore writing for *The New York Times* in 1969 called him "the first grim and gutsy pusher of social causes").

As the 1960s approached an end in the still hot exhaust of *Folsom,* American culture was bestowing social license on Cash. But his silence on racial issues, women's rights, and uncompromising statements of patriotism and faith may have been a lighted match to his social license, as well as to the national media's fascination with him. The same *New York Times* writer who dubbed Cash a "pusher of social causes" later in his article found his social fabric somewhat monochrome: "There is plenty of misery for Cash to interpret outside the prisons and reservations. The poor in this period of

With Folsom at his back.

(Photo by Jim Marshall)

richness are more controversial because they are raising a commotion and are disproportionately black. It has fallen to Elvis Presley to tell their story with Scott Davis's jumping ballad, 'In the Ghetto.' ... Cash will not talk much of the contemporary poor, of civil rights and civil wrongs, of black people and Chicanos. Perhaps many of the down-South country folk who buy his platters would rather not hear about these subjects...." The notion of crowning Elvis Presley a social critic was probably as laughable then as it is now, but nonetheless Dearmore represented the growing dissatisfaction with the country-based voice of the 1960s. Even the underground press cooled to Cash, put off by his undeniable conservative streak.

When the tuxedoed hero pronounced himself a dove with claws at a New York concert in late 1969 (an alignment with Nixon, in many eyes), it was like the country music version of Altamont, a bell tolling the end of the 1960s. Jack Newfield of *The Village Voice*, commenting on Cash's allegiance to the president, moaned, "A lot of us—Ralph Gleason, Nat Hentoff and myself among others—have been guilty, I think, of glibly trying to force too close an alliance between radical politics and rock music, to view the music as a surrogate for a political movement. We have tried to leech support and significance from groups, musicians, and lyrics when none exists."

In *Broadside*—where in 1964 Cash had courted the folk scene by so forcefully defending Dylan—a reader resentful of the singer's televised rendition of "This Land Is Your Land" joined the disintegration of Cash's newly formed fan base, while echoing Dearmore's criticism in *The New York Times*: "Cash, who seemed to be one of the most honest C&W singers, *used* Woody Guthrie's [song] in a bland, patrioteering manner which had nothing to do with Woody's meaning. Specifically, where in all versions of the song Woody stressed that this land belongs to the people who live in it, Cash turned it in to a mellifluous super-patriotic production—dripping milk and honey in a land of bloody Chicago, Black Panthers in jail and death in the People's Park, not to mention devastating poverty in its ghettoes and Appalachia and the unchecked pollution of its streams and airs."

Cash later distanced himself from Nixon and fired back with the protests "Man in Black" and "Talking Vietnam Blues," but it was too late to save him from the protest movement's divestiture. Those who had placed the mantel of national rebel on him, yanked it away, and in all of the pushing and pulling, the poignancy of *Folsom*'s political-cultural message faded. Cash's tenure on the peak of angry protest had burned out as quickly as it was ignited. By the 1970s, journalists were painting not a picture of a social commentator but rather a man cozy in the slipper of fame. In many ways, it was an apt rendering.

At Folsom came to stand over the years as a testament to Cash's own 1960s rebellion and lawlessness (read: drug use and other reckless pursuits) rather than the broader statement reflecting the spirit of the 1960s that it was. As a quintessential album of the 1960s, it didn't hold up to *Sgt. Pepper's Lonely Heart's Club Band, Pet Sounds, Are You Experienced?, Blonde on Blonde, Surrealistic Pillow,* and a handful of others (*The Band, Live at the Apollo, Bayou Country, Revolver, John Wesley Harding*). Ask people to name *the* top albums of the 1960s and few will include *Johnny Cash At Folsom Prison* on their list. It remains absent from the hallowed circle of pop albums produced when the album as art and social statement reached its zenith. It cries out for a place among the very top-echelon albums of that turbulent decade, shoulder to shoulder with *Pet Sounds* (1966), *Sgt. Pepper's* (1967), and the rest.

Albums such as *Pet Sounds* and *Pepper's* that so deeply marked the 1960s did so by either experimenting with sound and lyrics or capturing the decade's spirit of reinvention ... or both. Both fused various musical styles (symphonic, swing, rock, Indian) and tendered an acid-injected, surrealistic view of the world. In that they were social statements, they were because Brian Wilson's *Pet Sounds* lyrics had elegantly captured the yearning and uncertainty of youth, as did *Sgt. Pepper's,* particularly on the cut "She's Leaving Home."

Fusing sound also were Credence Clearwater Revival's *Bayou Country* (1969) and The Band's self-titled LP (recorded in 1969 but released in 1970). Both widely lauded outings, they issued powerful, hypnotic musical statements that honored the Memphis-to-Muscle Shoals rhythm and blues, the Memphis-to-Chicago blues of Muddy Waters and Howlin' Wolf, as well as the liquor-soaked hillbilly music of father Hank Williams. In distilling their influences, CCR and The Band solidly embodied the blues and country that is rock and roll (which, beyond its musical message, is a potent declaration in and of itself on race in America). Like *Bayou Country* and *The Band*, all of the great ones are held up as examples of different aspects of musical achievement and social import: *Sgt. Pepper's* and *Pet Sounds* for their innovative arrangements, James Brown's *Live at the Apollo* (1963) for its unapologetic assertion of black power in the decade of black power, *Blonde on Blonde* (1966) for its intricate and introspective poetry.

Ultimately, though, if we consider the '60s for more than its emphasis on experimentation and reinvention, focusing instead on the value the decade placed on solidarity with the disenfranchised in the spirit of Martin Luther King, Jr., Dorothy Day, Robert F. Kennedy, and others, close scrutiny reveals no popular album more emblematic than *Johnny Cash At Folsom Prison*. Taking nothing from *Sgt. Pepper's*, *Pet Sounds*, *Surrealistic Pillow*, and the like, all of which smashed musical boundaries, held up to the boiling social-political cauldron of the 1960s, they become something akin to campfire songs, Saturday morning television fare. Much of it, at its core, was self-indulgent or "abstract realms of personal experience," to quote folk-rock chronicler Richie Unterberger describing much of Dylan's mid-1960s verse. The same can be said about *Sgt. Pepper's*. In a 1968 interview, Paul McCartney called his group's masterpiece "just a little magic presentation," revealing that the group had thought of inserting in the album "a little envelope ... with the nutty things you can buy at Woolworth's: a surprise packet." Theirs—Wilson's, Dylan's, Lennon and McCartney's, and the imitators'— were lyrics that undoubtedly challenged the listeners toward introspection of their own or, at the very least, bent the mind swimming in LSD, but more often than not they failed as commentary on the major social and political issues of the day. As Robert Shelton complained, a tired paisley formula coated the pop music industry: "By 1969, everybody had to get stoned and make it to Woodstock, cut a psychedelic album, proved they were disturbed by Vietnam by freaking out."

Although a few popular performers rose above the posing Shelton derided to explicitly address the downtrodden in song—like Dylan on *The Freewheelin' Bob Dylan* (1963) and *The Times They Are A'Changin'* (1964) and others—Cash took the stage in front of the downtrodden, rolled tape, and flipped a middle finger at the establishment, daring the label—his authority—to censor his substandard stage banter and jabbing the guards—the prisoners' authority—for their part in repression's story. ("Them mean bastards ain't they," he had chortled during the show.) Partly theater, it was just real enough, though, to fill a 1960s musical soundtrack bereft of more potent social commentary.

And while others recorded in air-conditioned L.A. studios or amid trays of jam, cake, and weed in London, Cash bellowed his statement in the dull-smelling, January-chilled cafeteria of a state prison. As a session, it was an all-or-nothing deal, even with the possibility of post-concert razzle-dazzle in the editing suite. "It wasn't set and tweaked and planned and arranged in a studio," observes Marty Stuart. "It was one guy, his heart, and his rough-assed band, and his guts sitting in front of the fringes of society. It was flying by the seat of his pants." Cash's tightrope walk over the curious, wound-up crowd spelled the album's uniqueness among '60s albums. It was as if Dylan had recorded his "Ballad of Hollis Brown" in a Midwestern grange hall, a driving dust storm outside, or if Billie Holliday had taken "Strange Fruit" to Greenwood, Mississippi's court house steps.

The influential studios of the 1960s where the major artists of the day recorded had become sound processors—save perhaps the soul and R&B havens of Memphis, Chicago, and Muscle Shoals—where producers used over-dubbing, artificial reverb, and multi-tracking with a glutton's penchant. In contrast, *Folsom's* four microphones plugged into a four-track recorder symbolized the recording's give-it-to-them-raw attitude, a throwback to the rough and ready, breaking-from-the-cotton-fields spirit of Sun Records. Sonically, *Folsom* was a scratchy record, its sparse production distinguishing it from the crème of 1960s albums.

And in that scratchiness there is another dimension to the album's solidarity with the downtrodden. Cash could have remained home in Tennessee and recorded a prison concept album of prison ballads in the comfort and aural purity of the Columbia Nashville studios on 16TH Avenue (like Porter Wagoner, who recorded the classic LP *Soul of a Convict* for RCA in 1967). But Cash chose to be in Folsom, in its dank buildings, among its hungry prisoners. It never would have worked any other way.

The knighted albums of 1960s popular music—whether blues, country, or rock—reclaimed rock and roll from the Brill Building, Elvis soundtracks, and Frankie-and-Annette candy corn, pushing the once audacious genre to a new level of maturity while, in some cases, reminding the genre of its roots. But Cash did all that and one better: His album created a visceral social statement for the ages, one like no other uttered in the 1960s.

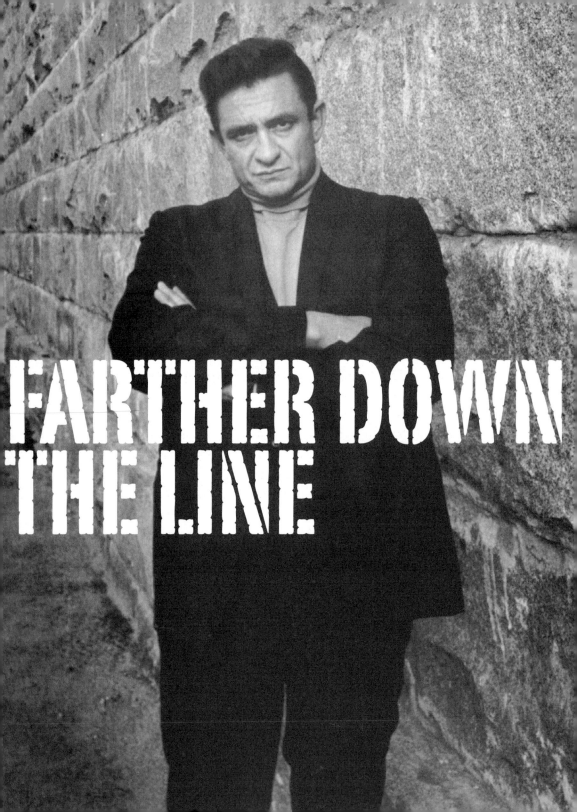

FARTHER DOWN
THE LINE

This mountain of memories is tipping
Its hat to the fall of the snow. — Denise Gasiorowski

0005

Although *Folsom*'s vehement 1960s statement soon dissipated in the public's eye, the album was sturdier in proclaiming Johnny Cash's fame. Before *Folsom* he was the great country singer; after, he was the great entertainer whose roots lay in country music and rock, even. "That's where things really started for me again," he told a journalist, although "erupted" may have been a more appropriate verb than "started." "Our career needed something," echoes Marshall Grant. "It was the album *Folsom Prison*."

Cash's catalog of recordings felt the first big jolt from the *Folsom* temblor. Enthusiasts sought out his old Sun and Columbia recordings, a demand to which Sun, particularly, responded like a salt merchant on an icy day. Cash's old label—purchased by veteran A&R man Shelby F. Singleton six months after *Folsom*'s release—repackaged Cash's golden years with astonishing fervor. The reception was loud, if you don't count Cash and Columbia, which found the releases of old material an irritant. Within a year of *Folsom* going gold, Sun uncorked a string of LPs, and, to rip off the aura of Cash's prison show, dubbed in applause on a reissue of Cash's 1956 classic "Get Rhythm." Buyers lapped up the recycled product, pushing the albums into the country and pop charts. Even the tampered-with "Get Rhythm" (released in the fall of 1969) managed to reach #23 country and #60 pop. Of course, sales of the superstar's new recordings post-*Folsom* also percolated. His immediate follow-up, *Holy Land,* sold significantly more than the industry's average gospel album, and subsequent albums moved briskly, too.

Then the ticket buyers swarmed out of the thicket. Marshall Grant figures the audiences tripled. "When *Folsom Prison* was let out, let's say three months from the time it was released, we were selling out every building in the United States or in the world, some of these huge buildings. You hear all

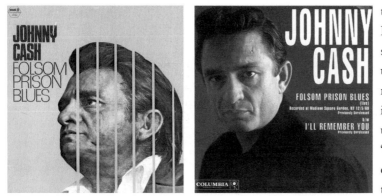

(left) Budget Pickwick LP inspired by *At Folsom*.

(right) Special 45 RPM of "Folsom Prison Blues" recorded at Madison Square Garden in 1969, released in 2002.

this stuff about Garth Brooks and other people sellin' 'em out in 18 minutes. We sold 'em out, but not in 18 minutes. Because in those days you walked up to the window and said, 'Give me two. Give me one.' It would take a week, ten days, to sell some of those places out.... When that album broke, everything blew sky high, and everything in our life turned around: our way of travel, our way of life, our concerts, everything turned completely around."

And then everything turned around two or three more times again. To exploit the Folsom frenzy, Columbia and Cash released *Johnny Cash at San Quentin,* a live concert performed at the San Francisco-area prison on February 24, 1969. One might have guessed that the sheer crassness of attempting to re-create *Folsom* would doom the album, but far from it. The startlingly uncreative concept rocketed into the popular music realm at a rate far speedier than *Folsom*'s; it spent a formidable 22 weeks at number one on the country charts and four weeks at number one on the pop charts, and it spawned "A Boy Named Sue," a top seller and another career song for Cash. Many, though, including Marty Stuart, see *San Quentin* as more contrived than *Folsom,* and therefore not as potent a moment. "Here's where you can see the difference in something that happened very naturally and then, 'Hey, that worked. Let's go try it again.' If you compare *San Quentin* … to *Folsom, Folsom* is a much more honest record because at San Quentin he knew all the right things to say; he knew what buttons to punch…. They probably shoved a little more canned applause [on *San Quentin*]. They hyped it, but *Folsom* didn't need no hype. *Folsom* just happened, man. *Folsom* just exploded, and it was meant to be. God was in on the deal."

If *Folsom* charged Cash's career, *San Quentin* supercharged it. Still, though, it had spun off of what Folsom had set in motion. When *San Quentin* hit warp speed, it did so in the still gusting draft winds of *Folsom.* Thanks to *Folsom,* Cash became a television personality, introducing his *Johnny Cash Show* in 1969 on ABC around the same time *San Quentin* debuted on the album charts. The show proved to be the electronic centerpiece of Cash's new career. Around it clamored the eyes of biographers and documentary cameras, marketers seeking his endorsement, loud fans in big halls, and ongoing press attention. "The smart money says *The Johnny Cash Show* is the one to watch," chimed the *National Observer.* "And the reason, simply, is Johnny Cash."

Fidgety in the glaring spotlight of international attention, particularly television attention, Cash pressed forward into the crush of fame, bewildered all the while that a gig in Folsom's granite city had made it so. "I've always thought it ironic," wrote Cash in his second autobiography, "that it was a prison concert, with me and the convicts getting along just as fellow rebels, outsiders, and miscreants should, that pumped up my marketability to the point where ABC thought I was respectable enough to have a weekly network TV show."

Respectability was certainly one of the bejeweled chalices that *Folsom* bought, but along with it came redefinition. Marty Stuart: "It recreated him, set him up for the '70s. It took him from being a drug-ridden has-been in the '60s (and at his worst he was always interesting). At the same time, I think it set him up as a pop culture icon. It really cemented the champion of the underdog bit, which is true. You know, there's nothing like success to get executives to pay attention to you. I think it made people pay attention again. He wasn't just another Nashville artist turning out quirky records. He was something to be reckoned with again." Was Cash not something to be reckoned with before *Folsom?* In the eyes of many at the time, probably not. His label thought it knew better than to expect extraordinary sales from him, and observers, at the label and elsewhere, would not have been surprised to see Cash flare out on a Hank Williams jag.

It's difficult to imagine just where Cash would have gone without *Folsom* in his guitar case. One critic speculated that he "faced a middle age of playing two-bit roadhouses for declining audiences and diminishing returns." Certainly, though, his Country Music Hall of Fame career had been secured in the stanzas of "I Walk the Line" and "Ring of Fire," but in the absence of 1968's conflagration, when Cash's hunch about a prison recording collided with the public's hunger for innovative sounds and rebellious outcries, his may have remained strictly a country career. His waltzes with Dylan may have remained largely a secret tryst without the light of *Folsom* to alert the rock and folk audiences who ultimately got behind the album. And similarly, his rock credentials issued in the Sun years may have cracked and scattered without *Folsom* to bring them back into full view. Would he have found another way to push out the borders of his acceptance?

And how does one measure the album's bearing on Cash's spirit? Was his marriage to June in 1968, the birth of his son John Carter in 1970, or recommitment to God enough to alone or together buoy him and massage his self-esteem? Or did the affirmation *Folsom* bestowed alleviate his interminable battle with drugs and ego? In a world without *Folsom,* does a second ghost from the vaults of Sun Records flit above the Memphis night in the

1970s, pausing—those two black-haired phantoms—over Sam Phillips' old storefront studio?

Such speculation could carry on forever, but Cash's career devoid of *Folsom* seems to spell mediocrity—at least in the years following *Folsom's* release. A reasonable scenario has Cash's career grinding down much earlier than it did, in the late 1970s and early 1980s as the pop-country vocalists and new traditionalists galloped into country music, herding their forebears to the carnival and riverboat casino circuit. Indeed, as Marty Stuart asserts, in the wild wake of *Folsom* there was a revitalization that would carry Cash to legend-dom and etch his name on the sacred tablet of 20TH-century popular music, next to Elvis Presley, Frank Sinatra, Bing Crosby, Duke Ellington, the Beatles. Dry spells appeared after *Folsom,* no doubt. But the album gave his career fuel to weather the droughts and reach the next redefining moment, the American Recordings era of the 1990s.

And what about country music? What did it find in *Folsom?*

Country music on *Folsom's* shoulders reached another climax in its long and fabled plotline. Patronized in the national media and reaching the end of the Eddy Arnold–dominated Nashville Sound years, country music seemed to be heading into the '70s with little soul. "It needed character," observes Marty Stuart. "It needed a kick." Offering rejuvenation, Johnny Cash roared a statement about country music's knack for commenting with stark realism on the human condition. It was a rousing re-calibration of country music, realigning the genre with its fathers and mothers: Jimmie Rodgers, the original Carter Family, Ernest Tubb, and other like figures. When Bob Dylan said after Cash's death that he was "the North Star, you could guide your ship by him," such was never more true for country music as when Cash released *At Folsom*. Country music's roots had been set on a course to the periodic revivals it has experienced in the decades since.

And just as Cash pointed country music to its roots, he led the genre in a dust-raising charge to new audiences. Country music's following and

The critical applause that *At Folsom* garnered in the late 1960s never really died. Journalists and historians in the years between now and then have continued to stand and clap, lifting ever-higher the album's vaunted legacy:

"One of the greatest, most electrifying live performance albums ever recorded; a hit album that effortlessly crossed over to the pop charts and made "Folsom Prison Blues," a minor hit at Sun 12 years before, into the song most associated with Cash, and a country classic, one that got as much airplay on rock stations as country."

—Rich Kienzle, *Country Music Magazine,* 1980

"His voice gets shaky in places and the band isn't always right there like it should be. But those are technical considerations, and this music isn't about technique. It's about presence, that intangible quality that only the best performances have—and usually because they're not performing so much as they're engaging in an act of communion. On this album, Johnny Cash is all presence."

—John Morthland, *The Best of Country Music,* 1984

"*Johnny Cash At Folsom Prison* remains one of the greatest live albums ever made. It sold 6 million copies, and extended Cash's fame beyond country music."

—Richard Harrington, *The Washington Post,* 1996

"He had stoked himself with amphetamines before he hit the stage at Folsom, and if the drugs made his voice raspy and limited its range, they added a rebellious glint to his demeanor—something that was apparent from the nasty way he curled his lip and spouted profanity throughout the show."

—Nicholas Dawidoff, *In the Country of Country,* 1997

"Performing in front of cons—a captive audience if there ever was one—was clearly something Cash cherished, and something he did often and remarkably well. He did it nearly perfectly on *At Folsom Prison*, one of the most powerfully visceral albums recorded, period. Americans bought the record in droves. When it was first released, in 1968, the Beatles, the Stones and the Beach Boys were all at their most psychedelic. Yet Cash turned a stark album of straight-ahead country rock into a bestseller, his first in five years. While the Beatles were singing about the love you make, Cash was earning cheers in Folsom by describing the impulsive, coked-up slaughter of his girlfriend on 'Cocaine Blues': 'Shot her down 'cause she made me slow/I thought I was her daddy, but she had five more.'"

—Seth Mnookin, *Salon.com,* 1999

"His music was the same as it always had been. Kicking off with his old Sun hit "Folsom Prison Blues" and following his usual formula of performing equal parts Cash originals and folk/country covers, he had the inmates of Folsom in the palm of his hand as his formidable storytelling abilities rose to occasion."

—Jim Irwin, *The Mojo Collection: The Greatest Albums of All Time,* 2000

"He was certainly in touch with his feral side that day, and enjoying himself immensely. The San Quentin gig ... was much improved—bigger show, better musicianship, superior pacing, etc.—but nowhere near as exciting. Helluva comeback record, *Folsom* was; the modern equivalent would be gangsta rap sweeping the Grammys."

—Patrick Carr, *Country Music Magazine,* 2002

economic influence had grown precipitously since the Second World War, when it was by and large confined to rural America. However, by the 1960s, Cash and other country artists regularly appeared in urban centers in the United States and toured widely abroad. But after *Folsom,* Cash ascended into a new stratosphere, taking country music along for the ride. Headlining at Madison Square Garden, the Civic Arena in Pittsburgh, Boston Garden, the Capital Centre near Washington, D.C., and in other similar forums in the years following *Folsom,* his shows, like his record sales, portended the coming of 1990s country superstars such as Garth Brooks and Reba McIntyre. There was simply no other country artist in the late 1960s drawing audiences as large and diverse as Johnny Cash's. More immediately, pre-Garth, he kicked open commercial doors for the superstars of the 1970s: Charley Pride, Loretta Lynn, and Willie Nelson.

Of course, Nelson represented along with Waylon Jennings the grimy Outlaw movement that both irked and invigorated country music in the 1970s. Cash never really ran with the Outlaws in their heyday, but, as *Rolling Stone*'s Anthony De Curtis pointed out, the movement along with the singer-songwriter movement in rock "provided him with aesthetic vindication and a raft of spiritual heirs." Cash was daddy to the Outlaw movement. He was the first country music singer to absolutely do things his way in the studio, refusing the hands of meddling producers. And when Cash lurched onto the Folsom stage, he became the closest thing country music had to an outlaw, this at a time when Willie Nelson appeared on an album cover (*Good Times*) in polyester slacks, putting golf balls with a leggy model, and Waylon was recording Richard Harris's unwieldy anthem "MacArthur Park" with the Kimberlys, a folk conglomeration. In the late 1960s, there was Cash to inspire Waylon and Willie's migration to stubbly fields where they found their classic albums *Lonesome, On'ry & Mean* (1973) and *Red Headed Stranger* (1975), respectively.

In the 1970s and 1980s, the artists whom Cash had helped reach broad audiences routinely outsold him, but nobody loomed over the industry like Cash. He was the legend, the living Hank Williams or Jimmie Rodgers, who gave country music its authority. If he wasn't always the biggest seller, he was the face on the genre, the defining imprimatur. He appeared more than his peers on network television; he got to produce his own feature film (*Gospel Road* in 1972); he led country music delegations to the White House; he toured abroad as easily as a country gentleman walking his acres. And where did this legend catch his stride? *Johnny Cash At Folsom Prison.* "It was the ending of the old covenant, before the new covenant," says Marty Stuart. "It was all those years accumulated of riding in cars and busting his way through rocks and fighting his way through black just to live.... The times got real good after that, monetarily and for fame and all that."

Amid the flush years after Folsom, on July 26, 1972, four figures—two lean rails, a bulkier man, and a small woman—sauntered through the cool marble halls of the New Senate Office Building in Washington, D.C. to meet the junior senator from Tennessee, Bill Brock. Cash, Glen Sherley, and Harlan Sanders, Sherley's former mate at Vacaville State Prison, were slated to testify on behalf of Brock's Federal District Offenders Board, a sweeping reform of the U.S. prison system. June, as always, lingered at Cash's side as they entered the hall.

The legislation was before the Judiciary Committee's Subcommittee on National Penetentiaries. Dwarfed by the high ceilings and the lofty committee seats in front of them, the three men—a prison trio—took their seats at the broad witness table. Silently, with grim countenance, they waited while Senator Brock described the bill's intention to eliminate unequal sentencing, and establish an advisory panel that would recommend standards for state institutions. Brock then turned to the witnesses, introducing the singer—uneasy in a jacket and necktie—and his two friends from California.

Cash had worked with Floyd Gressett on behalf of both men to win their parole from Vacaville (where Sherley had been transferred after his stay at Folsom and where he'd struck a friendship with Western Swing leader Spade Cooley, who'd been locked up for murdering his wife in 1961): Sherley, realizing the plan he'd hatched four years before to get Cash's attention and get out, received his release first in the winter of 1971, and Sanders followed just six days before that day's Senate testimony. They both had left California's penal system on Cash's promise that they'd be employed by his publishing company, House of Cash. Sherley had already written songs for Cash's catalog, recorded a live album at Vacaville, and joined Cash's never-ending road show.

As he paddled in the mainstream, Sherley came to embody Cash's dream for prisoners, that with human compassion many prisoners could find redemption. If all men were promised redemption by God—from drugs, from recklessness, from any sin—that meant prisoners too. So Cash had offered compassion, a job, a place to belong. Reading from hand-written notes, it was with that theme that Cash repeatedly pelted the committee that July morning. "Unless the public becomes aware and wants to, and wants to help and become involved in prison reform and really cares, unless people begin to care, all of the money in the world will not help. Money cannot do the job. People have got to care in order for prison reform to come about."

The senators—in awe surely of the shaggy-haired messenger and the two criminals at his side—listened while Cash recounted harrowing stories of rape and suicide in prison. His words packed authority that had grown from *Folsom*. Since the last ringing note of the 1968 prison show, he'd become the number one public figure on the prison reform question. And during the intervening years, the hoopla over *San Quentin* had only steeled his profile on reform as did his performances at other big houses: Lansing State Prison in Arkansas, New Mexico State Prison, Western Federal in Pittsburgh, and Cummings State Prison in Arkansas, where in an unfortunate spectacle he and Governor Winthrop Rockefeller had paraded around the prison yard in a donkey-drawn cart.

In media interviews, the sentient country star rarely let reporters go without lashing out at prisons and the prison system. A journalist traveling with the show in Texas found Cash—sounding a bit strung out—swinging with bravado about June and an upcoming album, and griping about the repressive air at Folsom in 1968: "You can't be in prison without being a prisoner," he complained. "They had guards all around with riot guns. Before and after the show, we were kept in the kitchen. None of the boys were allowed to see us." In another interview, Cash seemed more clear-headed as he preached about incarceration: "If we make better men out of the men in prison, then we've got less crime on the streets, and my family and yours is safer when they come out. If the prison system is reformed, if the men are reformed, if they are rehabilitated, then there's less crime and there's less victims."

Cash continued to speak out about and visit prisons throughout the 1970s—returning to Folsom in 1977. But then the concerts stopped. And Cash subsided like retreating surf from the reform discussion that *Folsom* had intensified. As the years passed, he saw a growing hostility in prison. Conflicts flared between prisoners who wanted to see him and those who wanted to see other acts. He ceased bringing June and the rest of the Carter Family, and fretted for his band's safety.

Disheartened perhaps by the hostility, which to him must have smacked of betrayal, and the failure of real prison reform in America, he laid aside his sword and banner. "He just felt that he had done his part for prison reform," observes Lou Robin, who managed Cash through the final 30 years of the singer's life. "And he started to focus on the other side of the coin, which was to help benefit the wives and children of police and firemen."

One wonders, though, if Glen Sherley's fate punctured his resolve on the question.

The connection between the two forged by "Greystone Chapel" had brought an extra wrinkle of significance to the Folsom concert, both in terms of the show's dramatic tension—as Cash realized that January day in 1968—and the way Sherley seemed to embody everything about prison that ran through Cash's head. With Sherley, he had looked into the eyes of a caged man and perhaps seen his own reflection. Music could be redemptive, Cash knew, and he believed it could be for Sherley as well; the songwriting prisoner's subsequent parole had been the beautiful denouement of the *Folsom* narrative, and a living breathing payoff in his personal prison reform crusade.

Grateful, Sherley joined Cash's show and sought new life on the outside for himself and others. "He came out of prison with a sincere heartfelt desire that he wanted to help the kid who hadn't gotten to prison yet," says step-son Rusty Courtney. "He wanted to save him from that.... He wanted to improve the world; he felt like he'd been given the opportunity to do something really special." In the 1972 Senate

Glen Sherley greeted by June and Johnny Cash as he arrives in Nashville in the early 1970s.

(Courtesy of Patricia Sanders)

testimony, it was Sherley—not Cash—who dominated the microphone, urging the senators that prison could be a better place, even unnecessary. They, the senators, could pull back the condemned from hell's threshold, insisted Sherley, as Cash had pulled him back:

> I was a three-time loser when John reached out his hand to me in 1968, and since then I sincerely believe that I have become a worthwhile person and can contribute to society outside as well as contributing to society inside.... If there was not any hope for a three-time loser, I would have been gone, because I was in Folsom and that is the end of the line in California. That is when they cannot do anything else with you, anywhere else, in the system and they send you to Folsom and that is where I was, and Johnny was and only that pulled me out of the muck because it made me want to try, it gave me the strength and the courage to try and only that. It has got to be concern and love and care. You have got to feel it and it has got to be from someone that you feel is worthwhile, too, otherwise it is not worth a damn. If it is coming from your immediate family, you do not know whether they are putting you on or saying, yeah, well, that is a good conning and you do not know whether it is or not because they are going to do that anyway, and the only thing that can help, the only way we can change it is with love and concern and care.

In the years after the Senate testimony, the gaunt ex-con wrote and performed and struggled to negotiate life on the outside, marrying an employee of the Cash organization, making his own home, and buying his own car (and wrecking several because during a life of incarceration he had seldom driven). However, his adjustment to freedom could not be complete; he gasped trying to comprehend the vast change in life, performing for huge crowds, moving shoulder to shoulder with the Hercules of popular music.

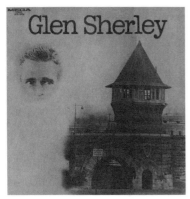

Sherley wrestled with the demons that bade him back toward violence, drugs, and robbery. He wondered how to be a free man. "My dad was what is now called institutionalized," says stepson Keith Sherley. "I mean, he was educated on how to survive in prison. Those rules are different. You judge people differently; you behave differently. He was taken out of the prison environment, California's last stronghold, and put in the spotlight. Now everything he said mattered. Everything he wanted could happen. That's a positive thing, but only if you know how to handle it.... You don't just make that shift without some type of rehabilitation. And rehabilitation was not a well-known thing thirty years ago."

Glen Sherley's self-titled LP on Mega Records, 1971. It reached No.32 on *Billboard*'s country album charts.

Slowly, like the building chorus in a Greek tragedy, Sherley's unease with his new life welled up in him. Home, he realized, was back behind the granite walls, where the crashing cell doors and the clicking boot heels of peace officers marked the passing of the day. On tour, he became much like the Johnny Cash of the 1960s, disappearing and reappearing, swearing on stage during shows that were now unabashedly family-oriented. The violent streak that dwelled beneath his rigid façade and intense eyes also possessed him with greater frequency—until it shook too many people on Cash's show. Marshall Grant: "I was sittin' in his room one day and we're just talkin'. I liked to talk to him because he'd been in prison almost all his life and I liked him to tell me stories about it. And he looked up at me one day with these hard eyes and said, 'Marshall, let me tell you something. I love you like a brother. I really love you like a brother. You've been so helpful with me.... I appreciate that.' But he said, 'You know what I would really like to do?'

I said, 'No man. What would you like to do?' He said, 'I'd like to get a knife and cut you all to hell. Let you lay there on the floor and bleed to death.' He said, 'Now that's what I'd like to do to you. But I can't. Unfortunately, I can't do that, so let's try to be friends.'"

Rattled by Sherley's confession and his increasingly erratic behavior, Grant took his worries about the ex-con to Cash. The bass player believed Sherley just might cut up everybody on the show. "John probably took that to him in some way ... and he and Glen, away from everybody else, had some words of some sort. And John just told him he couldn't travel with the show anymore."

One summer day in downtown Nashville, Bob Johnston was in his car when he spied Sherley on the street. "I said, 'Glen Sherley.' And he said, 'Bob Johnston.' I said, 'How you doin',' and he said, 'Everyday is Christmas.'" Nothing could have been farther from the truth.

Frustrated with Nashville, Sherley moved his wife and stepchildren to Utah, but almost immediately left them for the vagabond's life, traversing the country between Nashville and California, in a rusted, dented car, all of his belongings stuffed in the backseat. He and his wife divorced soon after he left, and when he returned to Utah for a visit, stepson Rusty struggled to recognize him: "He had a six-to-eight-inch beard, and just long straggly hair. He looked like a hobo.... He lived doing no telling what for a number of years."

Sherley continued to dabble in his writing and receive paychecks from Cash, but the fire that had implored the senators to find a way had dimmed. His addiction to heroin and other drugs, which had begun before his prison terms, snared him, pulling him farther down as his working relationship with Cash became a surreal memory. He often straggled wasted to the doors of old prison friends Earl Green and Harlan Sanders. "He kept going down, down," says Green. "He didn't talk right, didn't act right." He frequently threatened suicide, going as far during one stay with Green to slash his wrists. But he didn't die. He just lived like a dead man.

Few would have been surprised to learn that Sherley had landed back at Folsom. "And yet, I also believe that to have done that would have failed

Sherley at Folsom.

(Photo by Jim Marshall)

more than just him," speculates Keith Sherley. "It would've failed Johnny Cash, whom he loved.... It would have failed his family, and it would have failed everybody [to whom] he had said, 'You know, I'm gonna go out and show them that we are different.' ... And so it wasn't a choice; it wasn't an option." They met again backstage in San Jose, California, singer and mentor. And they laughed and hugged, forgot their parting. Sherley had settled back in the state of his youth and incarceration, and was staying and working with his brother, who was a maintenance manager at a feed lot near Salinas. But the move and the reconnection with Cash had solved little. He continued to weigh life and death, calling Harlan Sanders one night with another threat to end it all. "It was like an apology," recalls Sanders' widow Patricia. "He was sorry that he messed up all those years. Because he had the world at his fingertips."

On May 11, 1978, Sherley's brother got out of bed and left for work. Later in the morning, Glen awoke, walked to the porch, and shot himself dead. His brother came home for lunch and found him.

"A lot of people want to blame that on John," says Grant. "But ... John wasn't responsible for him. He just couldn't cope with the outside world. He really wanted back in prison.... But John gave him a good opportunity; he just couldn't fulfill it. That's all."

One hundred miles up the road from Salinas, as Sherley's passing was mourned, Sherley's former prison mate at Folsom Millard Dedmon allowed himself to think about life on the outside—breaking his long-established pledge to keep his mind where his body was. In the ten years since Cash had recorded at Folsom, the convicted kidnapper had faltered on the main line, finding himself hurled back and forth between Folsom and San Quentin after at least two knife fights. But he had reigned in his violent flashes and remained put at Quentin; there, after 25 years bouncing around the penal circuit and blowing his trumpet to stay cool, he had married a woman who lived on the outside and he earned an associate's degree. In the wake of sentencing reform that softened his life sentence, parole awaited him; a new job cutting meat at Hamilton Air Force Base near Oakland would be soon in

coming. On October 8, 1978, a few months after Sherley died, he walked from San Quentin's granite city a free man. Dedmon moved to East Oakland, and then resettled in Los Angeles. He never returned to prison.

Millard Dedmon blowing it not long before his release in 1978.

(Courtesy of Millard Dedmon)

NOTES

A NOTE ABOUT SOURCES

From time to time throughout researching and writing *Johnny Cash At Folsom Prison*, I tapped several general sources on Cash. Especially helpful were the late singer's two autobiographies (*Man in Black* and *Cash: The Autobiography*) and Christopher Wren's *Winners Got Scars Too: The Life of Johnny Cash*.

I relied on several sources to chronicle the history of California's American River Valley and Folsom State Prison: Wray Barrows' *A History of Folsom;* Robin Donnelly's *Biking and Hiking the American River Parkway: A Cultural and Natural History Guide;* Mickey Knapp's *The Branch State Prison at Folsom, 1856–1895: A Trilogy;* Jack London's *The Star Rover;* and Ed Morrell's *The Twenty-Fifth Man.* Various newspapers (the *Los Angeles Times, The Washington Post, The New York Times,* and *The Folsom Telegraph*) printed numerous prison-related stories throughout the 20TH Century. My picture of life in Folsom during the 1960s grew from interviews with various Folsom inmates and correction officers; Eldridge Cleaver's *Soul on Ice*—much of which was written in Folsom—also proved invaluable on that count.

To help me construct scenes from the Folsom concert, I leaned heavily on the photographs by Jim Marshall. Raw tape of the show from Sony Music's archives also gave form to my narrative; listening to the echoes of that distant event was a critical part of my research. Interviews with inmates and performers who witnessed the show as well as a *Los Angeles Times* newspaper account by Robert Hilburn contributed, too.

For information about the marketing of *Johnny Cash At Folsom Prison,* I turned to former Columbia Records' executives Wornall Farr, Tom Noonan, and Joe Casey, and I tapped back issues of *Billboard.*

INTRODUCTION

14   *Johnny Cash At Folsom Prison*'s unique and powerful: Among the sources ignoring *At Folsom* in top 100 album surveys are *New Musical Express, Q Mojo,* and VH1. *Rolling Stone* granted the album an #88 slot in 2003, sandwiched between Pink Floyd's *The Wall* (#87) and Dusty Springfield's *Dusty in Memphis* (#89).

CHAPTER ONE: TRAIN A' COMIN'

17   "To the impassioned will": Thornton Wilder. *Theophilus North* (New York: Harper and Row, 1973).

17   Six years earlier: For information about the 12TH Armored Division's first encounter with Landsberg, I relied on the 12TH Armored Division and the Liberation of Death Camps web page maintained by Abilene Christian University, Abilene, Texas (www.acu.edu).

18   "It was a pretty fascinating piece of equipment": Johnny Cash with Patrick Carr. *Cash: The Autobiography* (New York: Harper San Francisco, 1997), 58.

19   "The new picture gets mighty wrought up": Richard L. Coe, "Autobiography of Folsom Prison," *The Washington Post* (June 22, 1951).

19   "It was a violent movie": Steve Pond, "Johnny Cash," *Rolling Stone* (December 10–24, 1992).

20   "I think prison songs are popular": Dorothy Horstman. *Sing Your Heart Out, Country Boy* (Nashville: Country Music Foundation Press, 1996), 291.

21   Although Cash innocently borrowed: Author interview with Marty Stuart, 19 September 2003. Stuart related that Cash had told him about adapting Rodgers' line to "Folsom Prison Blues."

21   In the early 1970s ... : Author interview with Bruce Jenkins, 24 February 2004. Bruce Jenkins, one of Gordon Jenkins' sons, estimates the settlement to have been in the neighborhood of $75,000. According to Cash's manager Lou Robin, Cash acknowledged the influence of "Crescent City Blues" on his writing of "Folsom Prison Blues," but in the mid-1950s when the song was released he had been reassured by Sam Phillips that he had no reason to fear charges of plagiarism. (Author interview with Lou Robin, 16 February 2004.)

21   The inchoate lyricist: One struggles to excuse Cash's geographical lapses. Was Cash's prisoner in Folsom for another crime, the shooting having taken place at some earlier point?

22   "I really couldn't get my mind on anything but music": Johnny Cash. *Man in Black* (New York: Warner Books, 1976), 63.

22   The practicing continued "night after night": Cash, 65.

23   "There's something different about you guys": Author interview with Marshall Grant, 10 July 2003.

25   "His solo ... is one of the few times Luther ventured": Hank Davis, "Johnny Cash: The Sun Sound," *Goldmine* (December 20, 1985).

26   "John had his own way": Author interview with Frank Jones, 8 October 2003.

26   "I never did like musical bags": Pond, *Rolling Stone*.

27   "I'm trying to sell": "Write Is Wrong," *Time* (February 23, 1959).

28   "He was chameleon-like": Author interview with Harold Reid, 4 June 2003.

29   "I got hung, but didn't choke": Johnny Cash, "A Letter from Johnny Cash," *Broadside* (March 10, 1964).

30   "I was backstage": Anthony DeCurtis, "Johnny Cash Won't Back Down," *Rolling Stone* (October 26, 2000).

30   "Cash was hustled off to Baez's room": Robert Shelton. *No Direction Home: The Life and Music of Bob Dylan* (New York: Ballantine Books, 1987), 296–7.

30   "Closing the gap": Robert Shelton, "Symbolic Finale," *New York Times* (August 2, 1964).

31   "What's he doing here?": Peter La Farge, "Johnny Cash," *Sing Out!* (May 1965).

31   "Everything that Luther did": Author interview with Harold Reid.

31   "He could turn on to whatever particular audience": Author interview with Don Reid, 4 June 2003.

31   "The best of the modern country singer-composers": "Country Music: The Nashville Sound," *Time* (November 27, 1964).

31   "Great American voice": La Farge, *Sing Out!*

31   "Back-hill singers and strummers": "Country Music: The Nashville Sound," *Time*.

32   "The Opry House—the Ryman Auditorium": Larry L. King, "The Grand Ole Opry," *Harper's* (July 1968).

32   "Pallid, tasteless town": Gene Lees, "Nashville: The Sounds and the Symbols," *High Fidelity* (April 1967).

32   "Semi-literate tonic dominant strummings of itinerants": Gene Lees, "The Lighter

Side," *High Fidelity* (August 1968).

32   "Singular quality of realism": Lees, *High Fidelity* (April 1967).

32   "There were times we were very worried about him": Author interview with Jones.

33   "I got a lot of credit for it": Robert Hilburn, "Nothing Can Take the Place of the Human Heart: A Conversation with Johnny Cash," *Rolling Stone* (March 1, 1973).

33   "I got to where I had chronic laryngitis": Ibid.

34   "He is known as a song-writer and singer": Robert Shelton, "Troupe of Country Musicians Gives Program at Carnegie Hall," *New York Times* (May 11, 1962).

34   "There was several shows": Author interview with Grant.

35   "He showed up about daylight": Ibid.

37   "I'd had seven years of roughing it": Hilburn, *Rolling Stone* (March 1, 1973).

INSIDE THE WALLS OF FOLSOM PRISON:

20   "Warner Brothers, those inveterate": A.W., "The Screen," *The New York Times* (May 28, 1951).

THE TENNESSEE TWO:

24   "The ... instrumental style": Cash with Carr, 76.

24   Lapworth, Perkins told Marshall: Author interview with Grant, 10 July 2003.

24   "He couldn't turn it": Ibid.

CHAPTER TWO: STUCK IN FOLSOM PRISON

39   "You're starting fresh": Author interview with Jim Brown, 15 August 2003.

40   "After 'Folsom Prison Blues'": Sylvie Simmons, "Outta My Way," *Mojo* (January 2003).

40   At the time, nobody: Steve Eng in his biography of Porter Wagoner writes that Wagoner played a prison mental ward in the 1950s. It should also be noted that Sammy Davis, Jr. performed at Folsom Prison on December 16, 1961.

40   "By doing a prison concert": Cash, 38.

40   "He was supposed to be there": Simmons, *Mojo* (January 2003).

41   "Across the road on the Stuckey plantation": Christopher S. Wren, *Winners Got Scars Too: The Life of Johnny Cash* (New York: Country Music/Ballantine Books, 1974), 70–71.

42   "I didn't go into it": Paul Hemphill, *The Nashville Sound: Bright Lights and Country Music* (New York: Simon and Schuster, 1970), 100.

42   "From the very first prison I played": Peter McCabe and Jack Killion, "Interview with Johnny Cash," *Country Music* (May 1973).

43   "No one, least of all Johnny Cash": Donald G. Shockley and Richard L. Freeman, "Johnny Cash on Prison Reform," *Christian Century* (September 30, 1970).

43   "It takes no stretch": Peter M. Chandler, Jr., "Johnny of the Cross," *Christian Century* (December 2003).

44   "Its physical appearance is frowning": Ed Morrell, *The Twenty-Fifth Man* (Montclair, N.J.: New Era Publishing, 1924), 260.

47   "Convicts not hardened to endure": Morrell, 261.

49   Investigators in Cash's home state of Arkansas: Bruce Jackson, "Our Prisons Are Criminal," *New York Times Magazine,* (September 22, 1968).

49   "I can think of no prison": Ibid.

50   Recidivism rates across the nation: "A Summary of Humphrey Panel's Report on Crime," *The New York Times* (September 17, 1968).

50   "There is evidence": Dial Torgerson, "The Parolee—Can He Make It?" *Los Angeles Times* (May 13, 1968).

50   "Everybody had that old": Author interview with Millard Dedmon, 20 August 2003.

50   "Why should I want to leave?": Torgerson, *Los Angeles Times* (May 13, 1968).

51   "They thought I was sophisticated enough": Author interview with Dedmon.

52   "Years ago we had a young inmate": Author interview with John Moore, 20 August 2003.

52   "We built all the white boys": Author interview with Melvin Forbes, 20 August 2003.

53   "There was one incident": Author interview with Brown.

53   "We took care of, like, 250": Author interview with Forbes.

54   "The guy [who took care of the cat]": Author interview with Earl Green, 15 October 2003.

55   "When I first got there": Author interview with Dedmon.

55   "You missed cuddling with a woman": Author interview with Forbes.

56   "In your cell, you look up": Author interview with Dedmon.

56   "Folsom was a graveyard": Author interview with Dedmon, 19 September 2003.

CHAPTER THREE: BLOW MY BLUES AWAY

59   "Them poor babies": Michael Lydon, "Ain't Nothin' Too Weird for Me," *The New York Times* (March 16, 1969).

59   Law and Jones' big boss: "Executive Turntable," *Billboard* (March 2, 1968).

59   "Irascible opponent of studio executives": Howard Sounes, *Down the Highway: The Life of Bob Dylan* (New York: Grove Press, 2001), 185–86.

60   "He was one of those": Author interview with Don Reid.

60   Such speculation, though, is utterly refuted: Author interview with Bob Johnston, 30 October 2003.

61   "After six years of talking": Johnny Cash, liner notes, Johnny Cash, *Johnny Cash At Folsom Prison*, Columbia, CS–9639, 1968.

61   "I was sitting in the office": Author interview with Johnston.

61   "I guess I wanted to record": Wren, 218.

62   "That would have thrilled him": Author interview with Don Reid.

62   "We have seen him": Ibid.

63   "I remember I got a call": Author interview with Johnston.

63   They were, as former corrections officer: Author interview with Brown.

63   Cash's first visit to Folsom: Author interview with Green; author interview with Lloyd Kelley, 19 September 2003.

65   "We very seldom ever rehearsed": Author interview Grant, 10 July 2003.

66   Incarcerated on an armed robbery: Author interview with Kelley.

66   In Christopher Wren's telling: Wren, 218–19.

66   Born to Oklahoma farm workers: Author interview with Keith Sherley, 15 July 2003.

66   "He and another fellow": Author interview with Rusty Courtney, 15 April 2004.

67   "He was a typical inmate": Author interview with Kelley.

67 "It was a way to pass time": Author interview with Sherley.

68 "At that moment, Johnny Cash": Albert Govoni, *A Boy Named Cash: The Johnny Cash Story* (New York: Lancer Books, 1970), 29–30.

69 One of the guards: Author interview with Moore.

70 "Jim, there's a feeling of permanence": Author interview with Jim Marshall, 29 August 2003.

74 "It was an eerie thing": Author interview with Grant, 3 July 2003.

78 "Everybody was there": Author interview with Dedmon, 20 August 2003.

78 Only two weeks before: "Inmates Jump Guard in Attempt to Kill 'Fink,'" *Folsom Telegraph* (January 4, 1968).

78 Tensions were high: California Department of Corrections press release, 1 March 1968.

80 "I stood by the door": Author interview with Johnston.

88 "As relaxed as a bug": Cash with Carr, 201; author interview with Grant, 10 July 2003.

88 "They did what he asked": Simmons, *Mojo* (January 2003).

89 "His general demeanor": Author interview with Dedmon.

90 "I speak partly from experience": Cash, liner notes, *Johnny Cash At Folsom Prison.*

93 "It exploded": Author interview with Johnston.

93 "Let it blow": Johnny Cash, liner notes, *Johnny Cash At Folsom Prison,* Columbia/Legacy, CK 65955, 1999.

93 "You could feel it": Author interview with Grant, 3 July 2003.

96 "The guy was on fire": Author interview Stuart.

96 Luther's and Carl's licks: Seth Mnookin, "Sharps and Flats," *salon.com* (October 22, 1999).

96 "It's like a football team": Author interview with Grant.

101 "I gave them a stiff shot": Lydon, *The New York Times* (March 16, 1969).

101 "I was afraid of what they might say": Author interview with Grant.

115 At some point near their: Lydon, *The New York Times* (March 16, 1969).

118 "[He] may have been a prisoner": Author interview with Grant, 10 July 2003.

118 Bob Johnston cut from it: Cash scholar Frederick Danker wrote that Cash's Folsom Prison rendering of "Give My Love to Rose" was never so poignantly delivered. "Utter desolation," he observed. Frederick E. Danker, "Johnny Cash: A Certain Tragic Sense of Life," *Sing Out!* (September/October 1969).

118 "When you comin' back": Robert Hilburn, "Johnny Cash Records Behind the Walls of Folsom," *Los Angeles Times* Calendar (February 11, 1968).

119 "It was a great day": Author interview with Grant, 3 July 2003.

WALK THAT LINE:

74 When Bob Johnston learned: Author interview with Johnston.

74 Marshall Grant could feel: Author interview with Grant, 3 July 2003.

CHAPTER FOUR: GOOD BOY

125 "If you've got an image": Ray Coleman, "Rebels with a Beat," *Melody Maker* (February 8, 1964).

127 "What June did for me," Cash with Carr, 233.

127 "For me to tell you": Author interview with Joe Casey, undated.

132 "We never had what we thought": Author interview with Wornall Farr, 4 October 2003.

132 "He wasn't considered a sure bet": Author interview with Tom Noonan, 8 October 2003.

132 "It wasn't viewed": Author interview with Farr.

132 Nashville A&R man: Author interview with Jones.

133 If the label arranged radio: Author interview with Farr.

133 "After dinner we all got": Author interview with Noonan.

134 The *Los Angeles Times'* Tom Nolan: Tom Nolan, "How Goes It Underground?", *Los Angeles Times West Magazine* (February 18, 1968).

134 Peter C. Cavanaugh, of WTAC Detroit: Peter C. Cavanaugh, *Local DJ: A Rock 'N' Roll History* (Xlibris Corporation, 2001), 91.

135 Within days of Cash's new release: Richard Goldstein, "Pop Eye," *Village Voice* (June 6, 1968); Jann Wenner, "Country Tradition Goes to Heart of Dylan Songs," *Rolling Stone* (May 25, 1968).

137 The record's momentum flagging: Author interview with Noonan.

138 One—a front page cube: Columbia advertisement in *Billboard* (June 22, 1968).

138 "Underground was appealing": Author interview with Noonan.

140 Rumors of Cash's supposed time: Columbia advertisement in *Rolling Stone* (July 20, 1968).

142 He uttered them unconsciously: Dorothy Gallagher, "Johnny Cash: I'm Growing, I'm Changing, I'm Becoming," *Redbook* (August 1971).

142 Skimming Cash from the rest: Alfred Aronowitz, "Music Behind the Bars: Johnny Cash At Folsom Prison," *Life* (August 16, 1968).

142 *Time* magazine contributed: "Empathy in the Dungeon," *Time* (August 30, 1968).

144 His image grew more: Wenner, *Rolling Stone* (May 25, 1968).

144 Wenner's article, printed: "THE NEW BOB DYLAN: A LITTLE LIKE JOHNNY CASH?," *Rolling Stone* (April 6, 1968).

142 Tom Dearmore writing for *The New York Times*: Thomas Dearmore, "First Angry Man of Country Singers," *New York Times Magazine* (September 21, 1969).

145 The same *New York Times* writer: Ibid.

148 Jack Newfield of *The Village Voice*: Jack Newfield, "My Back Pages," *Village Voice* (December 25, 1969).

148 In *Broadside*—where in 1964: R. Padilla, letter to the editor, *Broadside* (August/September 1969).

150 Much of it, at its core: Richie Unterberger, *Eight Miles High: Folk-Rock's Flight from Haight-Ashbury to Woodstock* (San Francisco: Backbeat Books, 2003), ix.

150 In a 1968 interview: Alan Aldridge, "Paul McCartney's Guide to the Beatles' Songbook," *Los Angeles Times West Magazine* (January 14, 1968).

150 As Robert Shelton complained: Shelton, 457.

151 "It wasn't set and tweaked": Author interview with Stuart.

THE CRITICS, THEN:

140 "They're the ones": Author interview with Grant, 3 July 2003.

140 "Cash's voice is as thick": Goldstein, *Village Voice* (June 6, 1968).

140 "All the excitement": Robert Hilburn, "Pop Record Briefs," *Los Angeles Times* (June 16, 1968).

140 "This new album": Tom Henry, "Cell Soul," *Washington Free Press* (June 24-July 3, 1968).

141 "Now, out of Johnny Cash's": Aronowitz, *Life* (August 16, 1968).

141 "The Folsom album seems": *Time* (August 30, 1968).

141 "Every cut is special": Annie Fisher, "Riffs," *Village Voice* (October 17, 1968).

141 "Good basic performance": Donald Heckman, "In the Pop Bag," *American Record Guide* (December 1968).

141 "For not only is the album": Danker, *Sing Out!* (September/October 1969).

CHAPTER FIVE: FARTHER DOWN THE LINE

155 "This mountain of memories is tipping": Denise Gasiorowski, "In Need of Redemption," from *Mental Whatever* (self-published, 2003).

155 "That's where things": Hilburn, *Rolling Stone* (March 1, 1973).

155 "Our career needed something": Author interview with Grant.

156 Marshall Grant figures: Ibid.

157 "Here's where you can see": Author interview with Stuart.

157 "The smart money says": "Smart Money Says Johnny Cash Is the One to Watch This Year," *National Observer* (June 2, 1969).

157 "I've always thought it ironic": Cash with Carr, 201.

158 "It recreated him": Author interview with Stuart.

158 One critic speculated: Jim Irvin, ed., *The Mojo Collection: The Greatest Albums of All Time* (Edinburgh, U.K.: Mojo Books, 2000), 133.

159 "It needed character": Author interview with Stuart.

159 When Bob Dylan said: Bob Dylan, "Bob Dylan's Statement on Johnny Cash," *www.bob-dylan.com* (September 26, 2003).

161 Cash never really ran: Anthony DeCurtis, *Rolling Stone* (October 26, 2000).

162 "It was the ending": Author interview with Stuart.

163 "Unless the public becomes aware": U.S. Cong., Senate, Subcommittee on National Penitentiaries of the Committee on the Judiciary, *Parole Legislation,* 92nd Cong., 2nd Sess., S. 2383, S. 2462, S. 2955, S. 3185, S. 3674 (Washington, D.C.: GPO, 1972.), 71.

163 A journalist traveling with: Lydon, *The New York Times* (March 16, 1969).

164 In another interview: McCabe and Killion, *Country Music* (May 1973).

164 "He just felt that": Author interview with Lou Robin, 20 August 2003.

165 "He came out of prison": Author interview with Courtney.

165 "I was a three-time loser": U.S. Cong., Senate, Subcommittee on National Penitentiaries of the Committee on the Judiciary, 84.

166 "My dad was what": Author interview with Sherley.

166 "I was sittin' in his room": Author interview with Grant.

167 Rattled by Sherley's confession: Author interview with Grant, 10 July 2003.

167 One summer day: Author interview with Johnston.

167 Frustrated with Nashville: Author interview with Courtney.

167 "He kept going down, down": Author interview with Green.

167 "And yet, I also": Author interview with Sherley.

168 "It was like an apology": Author interview with Patricia Sanders, 14 October 2003.

169 On May 11, 1978: Author interview with Sherley.

169   "A lot of people": Author interview with Grant, 3 July 2003.

169   In the ten years since: Author interview with Dedmon.

THE CRITICS, LATER:

160   "One of the greatest": Rich Kienzle, "Johnny Cash's Greatest Hits," *Country Music Magazine* (July/August 1980).

160   "His voice gets shaky": John Morthland, *The Best of Country Music* (Garden City, N.Y.: Dolphin, 1984), 295.

160   "*Johnny Cash At Folsom Prison*": Richard Harrington, "Walking the Line," *Washington Post* (December 8, 1996).

160   "He had stoked himself": Nicholas Dawidoff, *In the Country of Country: A Journey to the Roots of American Music* (New York: Vintage, 1998), 189–90.

160   "Performing in front of cons": Seth Mnookin, *salon.com* (October 29, 1999).

160   "His music was the same": Irwin, 133.

160   "He was certainly in touch": Patrick Carr, "Caught in the Act," *Country Music* (June/July 2002).

BIBLIOGRAPHY

Barrows, Wray. *A History of Folsom,* first printing, fourth edition. Self-published, 1999.

Bogdanov, Vladimir, Chris Woodstra and Steve Erlewine, eds. *All Music Guide to Country*, 2ND edition. San Francisco: Backbeat Books, 2003.

Cantwell, David and Bill Friskics-Warren. *Heartaches by the Number: Country Music's 500 Greatest Singles.* Nashville: Vanderbilt University Press/Country Music Foundation Press, 2003.

Cash, Cindy. *The Cash Family Scrapbook.* New York: Crown, 1997.

Cash, Johnny. *Man in Black.* Grand Rapids, Mich.: Zondervan Press, 1975.

Cash, Johnny with Patrick Carr. *Cash: The Autobiography.* New York: HarperSanFrancisco, 1997.

Cavanaugh, Peter C. *Local DJ: A Rock 'N' Roll History.* Xlibris Corporation, 2001.

Cleaver, Eldridge. *Soul on Ice.* New York: Delta, 1968.

Dawidoff, Nicholas. *In the Country of Country: A Journey to the Roots of American Music.* New York: Pantheon Books, 1977.

Doggett, Peter. *Are You Ready for the Country?* New York: Penguin, 2001.

Donnelly, Robin. *Biking and Hiking the American River Parkway: A Cultural and Natural History Guide.* Carmichael, Calif.: The American River Natural History Association, 2001.

Eberly, Philip K. *Music in the Air: America's Changing Tastes in Popular Music, 1920–1980.* New York: Hastings House, 1982.

Einarson, John. *Desperados: The Roots of Country Rock.* New York: Cooper Square Press, 2001.

Eng, Steve. *A Satisfied Mind: The Country Music Life of Porter Wagoner.* Nashville: Rutledge Hill Press, 1992.

Escott, Colin with Martin Hawkins. *Good Rockin' Tonight: Sun Records and the Birth of Rock and Roll.* New York: St. Martin's Press, 1991.

Govoni, Albert. *A Boy Named Cash.* New York: Lancer Books, 1970.

Hemphill, Paul. *The Nashville Sound: Bright Lights and Country Music.* New York: Simon and Schuster, 1970.

Heylin, Clinton. *Bob Dylan: A Life in Stolen Moments.* New York: Schirmer Books, 1996.

Horstman, Dorothy. *Sing Your Heart Out Country Boy,* 3rd ed. Nashville: Country Music Foundation Press, 1996.

Hoye, Jacob, ed. *VH1's Greatest Albums.* New York: Pocket Books, 2003.

Irwin, Jim. *The Mojo Collection: The Greatest Albums of All Time.* Edinburgh, U.K.: Mojo Books, 2000.

Kahn, Ashley. *Kind of Blue: The Making of the Miles Davis Masterpiece.* New York: Da Capo Press, 2000.

Kingsbury, Paul. *Vinyl Hayride: Country Music Album Covers, 1947–1989.* San Francisco:

Chronicle Books, 2003.

Kingsbury, Paul, ed. *The Encyclopedia of Country Music*. New York: Oxford University Press, 1998.

Knapp, Mickey, ed. *The Branch State Prison at Folsom, 1856–1895: A Trilogy*. Golden Notes, Vol. 39, Nos. 3 and 4. 1993.

Lewry, Peter. *I've Been Everywhere: A Johnny Cash Chronicle*. London: Helter Skelter, 2001.

London, Jack. *The Star Rover*. Amherst, N.Y.: Prometheus Books, 1999.

Meade, Guthrie T., Jr. with Dick Spottswood and Douglas S. Meade. *Country Music Sources: A Biblio-Discography of Commercially Recorded Country Music*. Chapel Hill, N.C.: University of North Carolina Press, 2002.

Miller, Stephen. *Johnny Cash: The Life of an American Icon*. London: Omnibus Press, 2003.

Morthland, John. *The Best of Country Music*. Garden City, N.Y.: Dolphin, 1984.

Perkins, Carl and David McGee. *Go, Cat, Go!: The Life and Times of Carl Perkins*. New York: Hyperion, 1996.

Sanjek, Russell (updated by David Sanjek). *Pennies from Heaven: The American Popular Music Business in the Twentieth Century*. New York: Da Capo Press, 1996.

Sculatti, Gene and Davin Seay. *San Francisco Nights: The Psychedelic Music Trip, 1965–1968*. New York: St. Martin's Press, 1985.

Shelton, Robert. *No Direction Home: The Life and Music of Bob Dylan*. New York: Ballantine Books, 1987.

Silver, Sue. *Folsom Fables: Pieces of the Past*. Folsom, Calif.: Victorian Secrets, 1995.

Smith, John L. *The Johnny Cash Discography, 1984–1993*. Westport, Conn.: Greenwood Press, 1994.

Smith, John L. *The Johnny Cash Discography*. Westport, Conn.: Greenwood Press, 1985.

Sounes, Howard. *Down the Highway: The Life of Bob Dylan*. New York: Grove Press, 2001.

Unterberger, Richie. *Eight Miles High: Folk-Rock's Flight from Haight-Ashbury to Woodstock*. San Francisco: Backbeat Books, 2003.

Unterberger, Richie. *Turn! Turn! Turn!: The '60s Folk-Rock Revolution*. San Francisco: Backbeat Books, 2002.

Whitburn, Joel. *Top Country Albums, 1964–1997*. Menomonee Falls, Wis.: Record Research, Inc., 1997.

Whitburn, Joel. *Top Country Singles, 1994–1993*. Menomonee Falls, Wis.: Record Research, Inc., 1994.

Whitburn, Joel. *Top Pop Singles, 1955–1993*. Menomonee Falls, Wis.: Record Research, Inc., 1994.

Woodward, Lucinda and Jesse M. Smith., eds. (updated by William C. Dillinger). *A History of the Lower American River*. Carmichael, Cal.: American River Natural History Association, 1991.

WPA Guide to Tennessee. Knoxville: University of Tennessee Press, 1986.

Wren, Christopher. *Winners Got Scars Too: The Life and Legends of Johnny Cash*. New York: Dial

Press, 1971.

Zwonitzer, Mark with Charles Hirshberg. *Will You Miss Me When I'm Gone: The Carter Family and Their Legacy in American Music*. New York: Simon and Schuster, 2002.

INDEX

Numbers in **bold** refer to captions.